A Son from the Mountains

Also By Andrew Mossin

POETRY BOOKS AND CHAPBOOKS

Drafts for Shelley

From Blake's Notebook

ARC

The Epochal Body

The Veil

Exile's Recital

Torture Papers

Stanzas for the Preparation of Perception

The Fire Cycle

CRITICISM

Male Subjectivity and Poetic Form in "New American" Poetry

ANDREW MOSSIN GIVES US A BOOK that speaks with startling candor about international adoption. His own placement, from a mountainous Greek village of the late 1950s to the rapidly urbanizing American East Coast, set not only his own future on an unforeseen track but also the lives of his first mother and of his adoptive parents—trajectories of migration that do not ever converge again but that have, nonetheless, left deep, intersecting traces. Small nodes of contact, original documents, yellowing pictures, and heartfelt letters traverse lands and oceans but never deliver the closeness that a first mother wanted but could not give and that a new mother never allowed to take root. Mossin proves that, for many postwar intercountry adoptees, an unnecessary uprooting or adoption has come to mean a lifetime of adapting. Many will recognize part of their own stories in his, but few of us have found the poignant words and images in which to describe the never-ending journey.

GONDA VAN STEEN, AUTHOR OF *ADOPTION, MEMORY, AND COLD WAR GREECE: KID PRO QUO?*

TWO BROKEN FAMILIES, FRACTURED LIVES, prose that often reads like poetry and a deep understanding of what it feels like to be an adopted child, who experiences a complicated world beyond his control and of which he never really feels a part. This is Andrew Mossin's heartbreaking memoir, an adoption story that is raw, revealing and painful, about the presence of someone he never knew and the struggle to find his place with the parents who raised him. Although every adoptee's story and journey can widely vary, there are some constant refrains and some universal themes: Who am I? Where do I belong? Will I ever feel that I do? Without judgment or complaint, Mossin takes you on his journey, brings you into his world, and lets you experience it as he did. It is without sentimentality, but it is with an enormous amount of heart and honesty that he lays his young life bare. You feel for the child that he was and walk away wishing the story would continue so that his readers could know, after the challenges he faced as a youngster, how he prevailed and made his life the success that it is today.

MARY CARDARAS, PH.D., ASSOCIATE PROFESSOR AND CHAIR OF COMMUNICATION, CALIFORNIA STATE UNIVERSITY, EAST BAY

How do any of us survive being relinquished and adopted, even in the best of situations? Andrew Mossin documents in this memoir the experiences of living within a dysfunctional family that was ill prepared to raise a child. In so doing, he draws attention to the difficult integration of identity that any adoptee faces as they come to grips with the circumstances that led to their adoption and the family histories that arose as a result. I'm in awe that Mossin has not only been able to tell his heartbreaking story but has done so in ways that suggest the arc of a lifelong effort to rise above the claims of his own birth story and childhood. *A Son from the Mountains* provides important testament to the healing process through which Mossin has empowered himself to write and share, to shift the shame of surviving to the agency of honoring what one has lived.

    Lynelle Long, Founding Director, InterCountry Adoptee Voices (ICAV)

A Son from the Mountains collages recollections, alternately firm and knowingly unreliable, with the direct resource of family letters, and brief interludes of compassionate speculation. But the verb "collage" doesn't do justice to the seamless, lyric, and utterly compelling nature of Andrew Mossin's prose. The author accomplishes a feat rare in contemporary memoir: an immersive, meticulously realized understanding of daily life in households where love is a precious resource, measured and negotiated for under fraught circumstances. Those familiar with the neighborhoods of Northwest Washington, D.C., will find a whole other layer of resonance—and, as one of those people, I was deeply moved by this book.

    Sandra Beasley, Author of *Made to Explode*

a son from the mountains

A Memoir

Andrew Mossin

SPUYTEN DUYVIL
New York City

All rights reserved. Neither this book, nor any part thereof, may be reproduced by any means without the written permission of the author.

©2021 Andrew Mossin
ISBN 978-1-952419-94-2

Library of Congress Cataloging-in-Publication Data

Names: Mossin, Andrew, author.
Title: A son from the mountains : a memoir / Andrew Mossin.
Description: New York City : Spuyten Duyvil, 2021. |
Identifiers: LCCN 2021015935 | ISBN 9781952419942 (paperback)
Subjects: LCSH: Mossin, Andrew. | Adopted children--United
 States--Biography. | Identity (Psychology) | Birthmothers--Greece.
Classification: LCC HV874.82.M67 .M67 2021 | DDC 362.734092 [B]--dc23
LC record available at https://lccn.loc.gov/2021015935

To the memory of
Angeliki Sakkas
1932-2005

and

Iris Alford Mossin
1918-1971

Έχουμε μεγαλώσει μαζί

THIS IS A WORK OF MEMORY that relies on the methods of the fiction writer and the memoirist to represent events and experiences that occurred many decades ago and are not all of my own experience. While my effort throughout has been to remain truthful in this account, I have taken liberties in recreating certain conversations, scenes and other elements of personal history that have their basis in fact. Accordingly, names of individuals unrelated to my family have been changed to protect their privacy.

Let the stars of the twilight thereof be dark,
let it look for light but have none.
                                              Job 3:9

PROLOGUE

On a cool February afternoon in 1995, Angeliki Sakkas, a woman then in her early 60's, walked out of an office building on Mantzarou Street in Athens and headed toward Kolonaki Square. She took Solonos Street, then turned onto Kanari, a wide, level street with broad pavement preferable to the long climb on uneven ground that would have been required of her by other routes. She walked quickly past shop windows displaying expensive clothing and shoes for women and men, recognizing as she did so how out of place she was in this district of new wealth and commerce that had been developing since the 1960's and now represented the face of this newer, less affordable Athens. She carried a small shopping bag in one hand, while in the other she held onto her handbag as she crossed the busy intersection. Entering the square from Panagiotou Anagnostopoulou, she found an empty bench beneath one of the many bitter orange trees that lined the square and rested her weight against the back of the bench. The square was mostly deserted, few tourists coming to Athens at this time of year and the locals heading toward home from their work in the downtown businesses. Strong-boned with rough large hands marked from her youth working the fields near her village north of the city, Angeliki wore her daily outfit of dark blue-grey dress and a light blue shawl that was in need of repairing and black shoes with rounded toes, comfortable for long days spent on her feet. She pulled her shawl more tightly around her, as a cool breeze blew through the square. She again realized how out of place she must have appeared here, in this part of the city to which she rarely came. Angeliki's eyes, almond shaped and deep brown, still betrayed the hints of a smile now and again, though more often they communicated a sharpness and guardedness to those around her. Her left leg had begun to ache again from the phlebitis that had worsened in the last several years and she rubbed her calf with her left hand, as she noted the patterns of light cast on the ground from the orange trees that surrounded her. A few young people emerged at the entrance to the square and, apparently changing their minds, moved back into the shadows of Panagiotou Anagnostopoulou.

Stubbing out the butt of her cigarette on the bench railing and tossing it into the bushes behind her, Angeliki took from her purse the letter she had been given, still sealed in its envelope. She caressed the envelope's top edge as she felt the weight of its contents, holding the blue aerogramme envelope up so that the sunlight fell across its surface and shifted as the envelope and sunlight seemed to form one continuous band. *Paper and light*, Angeliki thought to herself, *paper and light*. As a child she'd been fascinated by what happened when objects caught the sun, how they transformed, became both less and more visible than they already were. The sun moved behind clouds as it dipped steadily into the west behind a group of apartment buildings. Angeliki couldn't say she had ever expected such a letter to arrive or knew what to do with it now that it was here. The letter sat in her hand waiting to be opened, as a kind of dullness entered her movements, before she found the courage to open the envelope and read the contents of the letter inside. She stared first at the English of the word-processed typescript, only a few isolated words and phrases of which she could understand, before turning to the Greek translation provided her. Each movement formed a parallel translation in her mind, Greek and English moving backward and forward as her eyes darted from one text to the next. The letter had taken two weeks to reach her from the United States via International Social Services, the agency that, 37 years earlier, had arranged for the adoption of her only child, Antonios. Reading to the end of the letter, she noted that his given name was now Andrew. Andreas.

She understood from his letter that he was about to marry for the second time. He had come to Greece in search of her years earlier with his first wife but had left without success, unable to find the family name listed in the phone directory in her village. Antonios was living in Philadelphia after having moved there from New York City, had completed his undergraduate studies and was now working toward an advanced degree. His Polish father who had emigrated to the United States two years prior to the ending of the Greek civil war in 1949 was now quite old and not doing well. Apparently, he'd been moved to Philadelphia to be closer to his son and lived in an apartment building across the broad avenue that led to the steps of the Philadelphia Museum of Art. Angeliki reflected on the coincidence of her own brother having been forced to leave Greece following the end of the civil war and moving to Poland in the early 1950's, where he'd remained to raise a family of his own. Odd, Angeliki thought, that her brother should escape to a country from which Antonios's father had fled so many years before. Returning to read the rest of her son's letter, she was able to glean few details from what her son related about the woman he was to marry or whether he had any children from his first marriage or would have any with his wife-to-be. The words were matter-of-fact with little emotion that she could read from what he had written—only that he expressed his love for her and his desire to see her one day.

When she came to the end of his letter, she read it again from the beginning, and did this three more times, each time moving back and forth between the Greek translation and the English, as if to ensure that she'd not missed anything. She wept through each reading, until some of the ink on the pages became smudged from her tears. When she had finished reading the pages of her son's letter for the fourth time, she carefully folded the letters into quadrants, just as they had been placed in the envelope, and sat holding the envelope in her right hand while stroking her calf again with her other hand. *Antonios,* she said, *my body is tired but my heart is filled with happiness to hear from you.* The words had failed her many times as she'd written such words down, then discarded them, having no one to send them to. The years had gone by...5...10...25....She had lost track and no longer spent her nights as she once had looking into the night sky for an answer to what had become of him. Sitting in the park, the light shifting to evening, Angeliki began writing a letter in her head to her son, Andreas, as she had done many times in her life, the letters remaining unwritten, parts of an archive no one would ever read. *Antonios,* she began, *what can I tell you, my son? What do I have to tell you now so many years after I was forced to give you away? Will you understand me when I tell you it was the hardest choice I was ever forced to make? That not a day has gone by that I haven't wondered, Did I make the right choice? What can I tell you, my dear boy. It has been hard here, very hard, there is little money in our country and little change since I was young in how I must work. Now I am tired but I must keep working, living as we all must. One is lucky to have enough, one shouldn't ask more than what you need. I have lived a long good life, I need only a few more years, a few more, until that day when you can visit your mother and we can sit as mother and son, as today I sit here with your words and speak to you, Antonios, that you might hear me.* It was an imperfect address she had begun, she knew this would need time to write, this letter to Antonios, and she bent down to pick up an olive leaf from the ground, something from Athens she could send her son with words, something physical and real, then let the leaf drop from her hand and listened again to the sounds of traffic outside the park as she rose slowly from her place on the bench.

Had she made the right choice? Her son had gone to America. His whole life had been lived as an American. What could be said about such things so many years later? Angeliki saw another elderly woman crossing the path, slowly entering the park from the same entrance she had come through hours earlier. Walking a bit unsteadily at first, Angeliki passed the woman and placed the envelope back in her purse and made her way slowly out of the square into the Athens night.

ONE

> Mother, I will go away. I will go away to a foreign land,
> far away to a distant land, and I will never return.
> Put on your black clothes! Put on you dirty clothes!
> Whenever I set out for home, I meet rain and mist;
> and whenever I turn back to that foreign land,
> I find sunshine and good roads.
>
> Greek funeral lament

Some initial facts: I was born at Alexandra maternity clinic in Athens, Greece, on a Sunday morning in April 1958. Not far from the Acropolis and the American Embassy, the hospital overlooks Vasileos Konstantinou Avenue with lush fig and almond trees in the courtyard that in the spring fill the air with their powerful scent. The moon the night before was a waxing crescent, the slim sliver of the moon's surface visible from the city center.

For the first several years of my life I wouldn't know the names of my biological parents or that they even existed: Angeliki Sakkas and Efthymios Kouroubis. At the time of my birth, my mother was 26 years old, my father 32. As I would learn much later when I was in my 40's, Angeliki had grown up in Liknon, a small village about 35 miles (or 50 km) north of Athens. Angeliki's mother died when she was barely in her teens, making it necessary for her to take care of her younger brother and sister. She would complete the equivalent of the fifth grade in elementary school before being forced to work in the fields with her father to help support the family.

When Angeliki met Efthymios, she was in her early 20's, living at home, still helping her father with agricultural work and supporting him in the care of her brother and sister. Her hair would have been dark as it was in photographs from later years; her eyes brown like mine. When she became pregnant with me, my father apparently refused to marry Angeliki. In culturally and politically conservative Greece of that era, this left few options for my mother. Conditions in villages like Liknon were such that unmarried mothers were considered "fallen women" and were shunned or worse by the local community. While her brother and sister were supportive of Angeliki insofar as they could be, she couldn't remain in her village and one morning in February of 1958 she boarded a bus to Lamia, the provincial capital, and from there took a connecting bus to Athens.

Angeliki would have arrived in the late afternoon at KTEL Bus Terminal B, on Liosion Street, a poor section of the city at the time but not far from her final destination: the Greek children's home, Metera (also known as the Babies Center "The Mother"). Built in 1953 at the behest of and with financing from Queen Frederica, Metera would have been well known to Angeliki as safe haven, even as far away as she and her family were from Athens. It was the only such place in Greece at the time where unmarried, expectant mothers knew they could find both shelter and support for themselves and their newborn babies prior to their being placed with families through adoption. The birth mothers who came to Metera usually stayed no longer than two or three weeks because of the center's high demand among unwed expectant women. The average time children remained at Metera before being adopted was roughly 150 days, while most would leave well before their first birthday.

For reasons I will never know, Angeliki remained at Metera well into 1959, leaving shortly before I was flown to the United States to begin life with my new family. While the specific circumstances of my mother's life at Metera can only be guessed at, what is most likely is that she worked as a housekeeper or aide to the nurses and doctors at Metera, receiving room and board for her work, no doubt due to her being viewed as a woman unafraid of doing hard manual labor. It's likely she would have been able to spend time with me during this period, though infants were quickly placed in the care of nurses who just as quickly became highly proprietary about their charges, viewing each of them as their own for the time that the children remained in their care. How might my mother have responded to that separation that was also a linkage, a way of staying close to her newborn infant while at the same time engaging in a process of weaning, separation, distancing that would take us away from one another permanently? The logic of that space, the illogic of another. I'm not certain she knew what would happen, even as it was happening; not certain she regarded it as separation so much as a pause in what the future would bring.

Photographs of Metera today show a two storey, brick and stone structure with a clay-tiled roof and a balcony that faced the almond trees across the driveway. Sometime within this period, I was christened in the small chapel that is on the grounds of Metera and given my Greek name: Antonios Sakkas. I still have the bronze bracelet I wore on my wrist with my name engraved and the date of my birth given as "20.4.58". It was this bracelet that I would have worn on the trans-Atlantic flight in June of 1959 from

Athens to New York City, roughly one year and two months from the morning I was born.

I can have no memory of those months I spent at Metera or those who cared for me, of their voices when they came to bring me from the nursery into the central activity room and, in the afternoons, was taken outside to rest among the other children in the newly-built playground. I cannot say what it was like to begin my days at Metera, how the light fell across the room at mid-afternoon that first summer when the heat was at its height, how many times during those first nights a nurse came to the room I shared with other infants, what the voices of these women sounded like, who would pick me up, what their arms felt like when they returned me to my crib. What I know is not what I remember but what I have been told, what I have found on my own.

These are the beginnings, then, of what was told to me, what I learned long after the fact, in other places and other rooms, at the hands of those who first knew me in the world. Many years later, sitting at a dining room table in a different part of this country from where I would grow up I would take out the map of Greece that Richard and Iris had once given me as a child and would trace out the path through the mountains in the north down to Athens and would remember as I did so each gap in the telling, as if the map's brown and blue shaded land masses were always at risk of being submerged under the green waters at the edges of each peninsula and island, as if inside each jagged cut of land there lay another edge, irrecoverable, dormant, outside ordinary time. And as I came down to the last layers of brown and blue, my fingers would trace out the figure of the mythical ibis, taking wing in another world.

TWO

We are who we are even when we're different, a good friend of mine once said to me. By which I understood him to mean that we remain the same person we always were, even when we change. A core of feeling, understanding, comprehension of the world that is unchangeable, even as much of how and who we become transforms over the years. Across the decades, retracing the paths that led this way and not that, to this life and not others, I've often come back to this single wish: to stop the film at any point along the way and start a new narrative, a new set of stories, resting my body there. What would the realism of that choice look like? *What if*, I've asked more times than I can count, Angeliki and Efthymios had married and decided to keep their child? What if I'd remained in Greece, grown up in that village north of Athens, lived out my life without thought of elsewhere, of other possibilities unfamiliar to my mother and father? Never thought of America except as someplace else, a foreign land, imposing its will on our small nation. What if...

*

In late 1957, my adoptive father, Richard Mossin, began inquiries into having a home study done by the Church Mission of Help of the Diocese of Maryland to prepare the way for an inter-country adoption of a child from Europe. This was the first step taken by Richard and my adoptive mother, Iris, to adopt, one that they initially had hoped would lead to their being offered a child of northern or central European background. As the documents in my possession indicate, it was no small thing for Richard and Iris, who came from white Anglo-European backgrounds, to seek to adopt a child who would resemble them in skin coloration; thus the search for a baby or older child from the northern regions of Europe. When no such potential adoptees were available, Richard and Iris turned to Greece, the one European country then in the process of accelerating its inter-country adoptions after decades of varied approaches to adoption, including the not uncommon practice of allowing for an "illegitimate" child to be quietly passed off as a child born to its grandmother or as the newly born baby of a childless cousin.

Initiating this process, then, would necessarily involve International Social Services, the primary liaison agency for such adoptions in Greece in the 1950's. Among many other steps that had to be completed prior to adoption was the home study that was meant to provide the ISS with sufficient information about the adoptive parents to decide on whether they would make appropriate adopters. In documents received from ISS nearly 60 years later, I have been able to trace the exchanges and sharing of information between Richard and Iris, the Church Mission in Baltimore and ISS that made possible their adoption of a child from Greece. Richard's letter to a member of the ISS staff in March of 1958 gives a good sense of the tenor of these exchanges as they developed over the next 27 months.

Dear Mr. Kirk:
As you probably remember, my wife and I visited you in New York City in the beginning of October last year, after

the initial approach had been made by our mutual friend, Raymond Houseman, in connection with the possibility of adopting a child.

We were encouraged by your sincere readiness to help us. We understood however, that nothing could be done by your office until a home study had been made, in this case by the Maryland Church Mission of Help.

We journeyed to Baltimore immediately after seeing you and made contact with Sister Benedetta, who, after the formal, preliminary investigation, assured us that she would come to our house in the near future to finalize everything, since only the home survey was needed to conclude investigations when all the necessary documents would then be forwarded to you.

Four months have now elapsed, and despite many letters and phone calls to Baltimore, unfortunately, nothing further has transpired.

We came to New York last February and visited with your office and spoke to Mrs. James in your absence, asking for any possible advice in Washington D.C. who might help us; in view of this we wrote to Sister Benedetta in Baltimore that if she found it impossible to visit us in Washington perhaps the home study could be undertaken by this agency. We have had no reply to this suggestion.

We are most worried that time passes without sign of anything happening.

Although we are reluctant to bother you, could we please ask you to contact your representative in Baltimore again or should we apply to the agency in Washington starting all over from the beginning?

Yours sincerely,
Richard E. Mossin

After an extensive back and forth that went on for several months, the home study was completed by a caseworker from the Church Mission in May of 1958. Apparently it was customary for outside organizations such as the Church Mission to assist ISS in doing such home studies, given the lack of resources on the part of ISS to do such studies themselves. Reading the home study documents more than 60 years after the fact, I feel like the character in the Delmore Schwartz story who stands up in the movie theatre and shouts at the screen images of his parents, "What are they doing? Don't they know what they are doing?" But what can I say? What they were about to do, setting out to do, was already in motion. The film was running…

The home study was done sometime in March of 1958, following a number of letters back and forth between Richard and the Church Mission. There were scheduling issues, delays as a result, and finally the caseworker came down from Baltimore to talk to Richard and Iris. It's impossible to say what that looked like, though in all probability the caseworker came out for a full day of meeting with and talking to Richard and Iris. A settlement worker, no doubt, with some experience in doing such home studies, she would have entered the row house on Ashmead Place in Washington and noted the careful arrangement of tasteful furnishings that Richard and Iris had brought down with them from their former apartment in New York City, as well as the overall neatness and cleanliness of their home. She would have been struck by the photographs of General Anders and other Polish military officers that hung over the fireplace in the living room and, not knowing the individuals pictured, would have surmised that they were photos of individuals important to Richard and Iris.

In the caseworker's account, Richard and Iris appear as "an interested couple who seem to have fitted themselves into the American way of life successfully. They are friendly people, and have made many contacts since coming to Washington. They enjoy their home and community, are congenial and seem to have achieved a marriage of normal adjustment and happiness." Richard and Iris would have been forty-eight and forty years old respectively at the time, older than would have been common for first-time parents, but nothing is mentioned in the report to indicate that the caseworker took issue with their ages. Richard is described as "a man who moves with military bearing, with blue eyes and dark hair." Iris is portrayed as "rather slender in build, with grey-blue eyes and dark hair. There are grey, blue, and brown eyes in her family, and all shades from a reddish brown to dark brown hair." These last comments are particularly striking for what they convey of the emphasis being placed on physical resemblance vs. temperamental qualities, as if my appearance among these strangers were of more significance than whether Richard and Iris were the best potential fit as parents to an adopted child. For religion, they are described as secular Christians, my father having been baptized in the Catholic Church in Poland and Iris having remained a confirmed communicant of the Church of England, while attending church infrequently at a local parish in Washington.

The study includes a description of the house and street where Richard and Iris lived, one that is characterized as a "quiet residential block of Washington, in mid-town. It's a dead-end street," the caseworker notes, "only one block long, and is bounded on the four corners by apartment houses.

The homes in between are closely built, but entirely separate, with their own back and front lawns. It is an attractive street with trees, and every home has its front lawn and flowers." The language has the detached yet polished quality of magazine advertising copy from this era, as if to say, *This is an American family like all other American families. They own the things we all want to own; they live on a street that looks just like the ones you and I live on.* Translation: this is a white, middle class American family with appropriate standing in their community; they pass the test.

The report concludes with this statement of support for moving ahead with adoption: "We believe that Mr. and Mrs. Mossin are very sincere in their desire for a child, and that they look to the possibility of an overseas child because of their own background. As far as we can determine, they will make every effort to meet the needs and handle the adjustment of an overseas child in a secure manner. We believe that they will do all they can to cooperate in an adoption plan and we hope that a suitable child, as young as possible, may be found for them."

On June 6, 1958, a Friday, my father wrote to the General Director of the American Branch of ISS USA in New York that he was happy to let the Director know that the home study had been finally concluded and that now he would "appreciate a few words of encouragement from you on the chance of your organization in finding us an adoptee, or perhaps you would most kindly communicate to me the name of the person in your office with whom I should be in contact."

In December, ISS Hellenic Branch sent a communication to ISS-USA that they had found a baby who might be a good match for this couple. The baby's name was given as "Sakas" and his birth date listed as April 20, 1958. A description of his development followed: "Sits for a few seconds with out support. Stands with help from hands and partly bears weight of his body. Turns to all positions, from prone to supine and vice-versa...He likes to have constant company and is very happy near the people he knows. Vocalizes, laughs aloud, repeats ba-ba etc. and continuously chattering." The document is signed "The Pediatrician."

In response to concerns that baby Sakkas's left eye suffered from ptosis, Richard and Iris contacted a doctor they knew at The Long Island Jewish Hospital in New York and he wrote in February 1959 that "he looks adorably cute and the ptosis of the left eye is hardly enough to make any difficulty. If it persists, surgery can be helpful at a later date."

ISS-USA sent an RCA radiogram on February 25 to its Athens branch with the following message: "MOSSINS AND AGENCY FULLY ACCEPT MATCH AWAITING CHILDS DOCUMENTS POWER OF ATTORNEY FORTHCOMING."

After several more exchanges of legal documents and letters, in which the possibility was raised by Iris of her coming to Greece to bring baby Sakkas back to the U.S. with her (this possibility was rejected when Iris decided to quit her position as manager of a local travel service to make time to stay at home with her new child), details were finalized for travel from Greece to the United States. On Tuesday, June 2, 1959, Antonios was flown with two other adoptees aboard a KLM, Royal Dutch Airlines flight from Athens to New York via a connecting flight in Amsterdam. Their flight, initially scheduled to arrive at New York's Idlewild Airport at approximately 8 a.m. EST, was delayed by several hours and didn't land until 11:20 a.m.

Richard and Iris, who had driven up to New York in a rental car the day before, were waiting at the gate when their child was brought down to them by the ISS caseworkers who'd accompanied the children on the flight. There had been steady rain for several days and when the 14 month-old was brought from the plane to Iris and Richard waiting on the tarmac below, the rain formed a light film on his face so that Richard was convinced that his new son had come to them with fever. Iris looked at Richard and said, "He has your mouth and eyes…" Richard turned away from her at that moment, both embarrassed and proud of his orphan son who had arrived in early June, a little less than two years after he and Iris had first considered the idea of adoption.

After lengthy processing by immigration, Richard and Iris thanked the caseworkers for all their help and placed Antonios in the stroller he and Iris had brought with them. Rather than drive back in a rental car, they'd decided it would be less stressful on their new baby to catch the next flight out that would return them to Washington. This would be their first trip together as a family.

Surname	Given Name	Passport Number
SAKKAS	—	5634
Nationality (Citizenship)	Birthplace	Birthdate
GREECE		

United States Address: 2305 ASHMEAD PLACE NW WASH DC

Permanent Address:

Visa Issued At:
Date Visa Issued:

Vessel Name or Airline and Flight No. of Arrival: KL 643
Passenger Boarded At: Amsterdam

IMM. & NATZ. SERVICE
NEW YORK, N.Y. 53
ADMITTED
JUN 3 - 1959
CLASS IJ

Form 194 A (Rev 7-1 57)
ARRIVAL-DEPARTURE RECORD

THREE

What were those first nights and days in America like for Antonios, soon to become Andrew? I have memories of spending my nights in a crib in the living room of the house at Ashmead place, of waking in the middle of the day in the shadows of that room and climbing out and beginning to make my way across the darkened space until I am picked up by a woman who may or may not have been Iris. At other times I am sitting in the low light of the shaded balcony that adjoined one of the bedrooms upstairs and I am looking into the garden below where my pet turtle lives and Iris's cats wander among the ivy and rhododendrons. There is a static, prescient quality to these evocations of a period in my life that is both beyond my recall yet lodged there nonetheless in images that come to me from photographs and dim sense memories that have remained in my consciousness.

And for Iris and Richard who had longed to possess a child of their own, then finally been able to do so? What did they make of the changes to their household brought about by the sudden appearance of this brown-skinned baby from Athens whose left eye drooped slightly and who hadn't yet formed his first intelligible words? The letters, now written by Iris, reflect what life might have been like at 2325 Ashmead Place in those first days following my arrival. This one, the earliest I have, is from June 8, 1959, five days after I would have arrived by plane from Athens. It was written to a representative of the Church Mission of Help in Baltimore, no doubt to reassure them that the

Mossin household was in fine order with the introduction of its newest member. The addressee is redacted in black marker, as is the case with all the documents I've received from ISS, to protect the identities of those named.

>Dear ....
>
>I know you will forgive me for not writing sooner, but since the baby's arrived every second has been occupied and I'm only now catching up on my sleep!
>
>Little baby Antonios is a darling baby; he is now happy, adjusted and content.
>
>I have to consider myself fortunate in that I have a wonderful nanny for him, and they adore each other.
>
>First, when we received him at Idlewild Airport last Wednesday, in the company of two charming young ladies from ISS, he appeared dazed—and even an adult wouldn't feel jubilant after journeying all the way from Athens to New York (oddly enough I made the same flight all in one day three years ago and I was exhausted). One of the young ladies told me that when babies do not cry and yell on their way over, reaction sometimes sets in later. And so it transpired: Andrew (Antonios) was as good as gold on the flight from New York to Washington, and whimpered a little during the cab ride home. For the next forty-eight hours, he cried and screamed and sleep was impossible for our little household.
>
>On the Friday, the pediatrician came and examined him and pronounced him 100% fit (tomorrow we take him polio shots), and he gave me some good words of advice because, at that time, I was completely overwrought. Nanny came the same day and I got some rest.
>
>Of course he still cries intermittently, but this is induced by normal things like teething, when he is hungry, when he awakes or when he requires a change of diapers.

He says: "Da-Da", "Ba-Ba", and, with difficulty, "Ma-Ma." He crawls with amazing speed, but he has not yet accomplished the feat of walking. He has a stroll twice a day, and has a wonderful splash in a little bathing pool which we have installed in the garden. I am having to keep him on bottles because he doesn't yet care for milk any other way, though he does try and sip his orange juice from a glass.

I don't mean to bore you with all these details, for they are exciting and I just got carried away.

The letter concludes with a series of questions for the ISS caseworker, among them for how long they will need to refer to me as "Antonios," when Iris notes that she and Richard would prefer to have me christened Andrew Richard Alford Mossin. In another letter from this same week, this one directed to ISS-New York, Iris writes that Andrew "just worships his father. When my husband is in the room, for little Andrew, he is the sun, moon, and stars rolled into one." I cannot assess the truth of that statement, but it's important that here, in the weeks following my arrival, Iris is already making note of this shift, this disturbance, if you will, of my father's affections that had, it seems, been entirely directed toward my mother until I arrived. Or that's the portion of the story that was repeated to me over time and became, as my mother's words would record it, something like a truth with the passing of time.

FOUR

Fourteen years separate the time of the month in which this photograph was taken from the end of World War II. My father appears with me on the porch of our first house in Washington, at Ashmead Place in the Kalorama section of the District of Columbia. He would be forty-nine years-old in this photograph. Bare-chested, wearing only his swim trunks and sandals, he looks down on the figure of a toddler wearing diapers and in the child's hands is a small rubber hammer and a drum. Behind them there is wild ivy growing in the garden and the trees along the street are in full leaf, mid-summer. The day must have been a warm one and by the looks of it we're moving past the mid-day point, probably around two or three in the afternoon, the sun high up and straight over us. Richard's gaze tells the story of his newly discovered role as father: his hand supporting me, vigilant, careful, wanting to be sure I don't fall.

In other photos from this early period of my life, there are few of my mother and none in which she and I appear together. Richard is the photographer for these shots, as I assume my mother is the one with the camera in these pictures of my father and me. It is past recall, yet I know that he is sometimes there with me and lies in the wet summer grass near the small plastic pool in the front garden and watches as I throw the plastic pail into the air and let it fall into the water again and again. One morning, the sun edging its way over the rooftops of our neighborhood, I am placed in the water and I feel his arms move around me, as he grasps hold of me and secures my body in the cool liquid. Later he takes me out of the pool and throws me up in the air. And it is like light and color are one with our bodies and his arms are beams holding me above him, and his face is like a beam of dark light on my face, when I come down again and fall into his arms and am placed in the cool water once more.

On another occasion, I am left alone for hours at a time, left to pull at the plastic ring of colored blocks given me by my mother one early morning and the two stuffed animals behind me that my mother placed there, and beside me are the small plastic boats I have been pushing from left to right in a serial motion that I can only duplicate in rhythm to the light beams falling. I imagine them encompassing my body in a sort of free fall of light and water, water and light. Inside the house my mother has started preparing lunch, while outside on the porch my father is making the gate to keep me from falling down the stairs. Upstairs in their bedroom, there is the sound of one of the cats moving, the other is not moving and has taken a position at the window. As I look up the light from the window sharpens, distills, and it's like flakes of sea grass falling from the sky, falling into my small pool, and I can grab at them but never catch them, grab onto them but never quite take hold of their edges. Later, my father will come to get me and put me in my crib, where I'll nap to the sound of the water flowing from the faucet in the kitchen, the birds moving among the plants on the front porch.

FIVE

Roughly ten years after Richard and Iris had moved to the United States in 1947 to take up residence there, my father tried to make an account of the most significant events of the past year: "In general it was another good and prosperous year for both of us. We moved from New York to Washington. I started a new ~~life~~ job which can called 'stabilized and secured." We bought our first house and we enjoy it. Financially, we did not gain very much during this year, but we invested our saving in the most secure object – ~~the house~~." From the same set of pages, immediately following my father's mention of the house: "We decided to adopt a baby. Of course there is a long way to the success of our attempts. But first steps were taken." The entries for 1957 end with this entry for December: "On X-mas eve Iris wrote to me one of nicest letters I ever received from her." The letter wasn't saved, so there's no record of what Iris wrote.

There is this channel running through their words, his and hers, this way of saying things that becomes a kind of silencing at the same time. "We decided to adopt a baby." That line, like a lure left in place of whatever else could be said. Iris would tell me much later—around the time that everything had genuinely started to fall apart, around the time of her first suicide attempt in 1968, when I was ten— that the reason they'd had to adopt was because she and my father discovered that she couldn't have a baby.

"We wanted our own," she said to me one afternoon in the fall of 1968. "Well, Richard wanted one very badly. God, we tried. And finally we went to see the doctor who did tests and they showed some problem with my insides. That was that, as they say. Took us awhile, but, finally, we got the agency that brought you over to show us some photos, and yours came up and, well, Richard was in love." Her voice revealed little emotion at the time, while at the same time, there was all that wasn't being said, about these beginnings, this approach to bringing a child into their world, as if whatever she said, she knew that she couldn't put it all into words or that the words would fail on their way, and she would have to start all over again, at the beginning.

"Richard was in love with his son, with you, I can tell you I've never seen him happier than the day you arrived on the plane from Greece. He had tears in his eyes, real tears, that finally he would become a father of a child."

When my husband is in the room, for little Andrew, he is the sun, moon, and stars rolled into one. There are gaps, to be sure, in what I have received, in what I can know. My mother that day she spoke to me would not have known that she had only three years to live or that her circling back to a sentence from one of her first letters documenting my arrival would one day find its way into that adoptee's hands.

Iris would have repeated what she knew. "You were everything to your father."

In that decade Angeliki, now in her 30's, would have worked as a domestic live-in before marrying for the first time in 1965. The marriage would end in divorce in 1970. In those days and nights she may have wondered about the son, Antonios, who she'd brought into the world those many years earlier. Sitting on the patio of the apartment she would share with her husband before separating from him and moving to another in the coming year, she may have seen the moon pass over the hills and understood that for the little boy another decade had come and gone as well.

Their lives were elsewhere. *My son from the mountains*, she may have said to herself, as if only God could hear her, *may he be kept safe wherever he has been taken.*

SIX

In that first back garden at Ashmead Place I had two small turtles, one with a grey-green shell, the other a bluish yellow. Each morning I would be brought out to the garden by the woman hired by Richard and Iris to take care of me. She would place me on the bottom step of the back porch leading down to the garden and I would sit and wait for my turtles to appear. It was sometimes several minutes before they did and as they crawled from out of the ivy bed I would wave my arms and point to them and using my first words call out to them, *Turwill! Turwill!* Our nanny would accompany me as I started to walk into the garden and picked up one of the turtles in my small hands and cradled it to my bare chest. *Now Andy,* she would say, *don't be rough with him, put him back down, don't hurt him, just let him go.* The turtle's head would have disappeared in its shell and I would wait for it to reappear but it wouldn't and as I watched from the floor of the garden as he rejoined the other turtle I would see the light coming into the garden through the trees, single spears of orange and yellow, and I'd hold the nanny's hand in mine and walk with her back into the house where it was cooler and the light changed all over again.

*

Richard and Iris couldn't have become whom they were without their having seen their worlds destroyed, not once but twice. Both of them were survivors of two World Wars—

my father born four years before the beginning of World War I, my mother one year after its conclusion—followed by exile in a country neither claimed as their own. America was just the place they came to, not one either would have chosen otherwise. As my mother used to tell it, she'd come over first to Toronto, had fallen in love with a city that was beginning to draw a significant immigrant population, as the city spread from its urban center out to a suburban landscape that was soon dubbed "metropolitan Toronto." But unable to find work there for my father, Iris had moved south, into the U.S. and New York.

"Richard was simply unable to find work, even on my good name as a journalist in England," my mother said to me one day after we'd come back from a grocery trip. I'd unpacked everything and put the cold stuffs in the fridge and come back into the living room, where my mother had opened a cold Old German bottle of beer. "So, we packed our valises, and one day we are on the Queen Mary and the next in New York City and beginning our life together here."

"Did you know you would stay?" I asked.

"What alternative did we have? Nothing for your father left in Europe, barely enough for me. But, yes, we thought we would give it a try. Poland was finished, Britain rebuilding but far from where it would need to be. We were part of that wave that came to America after the war looking for something better. Maybe we would be proven wrong—I would say, yes, in some ways, we were—but we had to try."

And if they hadn't come over, these two émigrés, survivors, but instead had remained in London and lived out their lives in Europe, never coming to this country, this city—what then? Or if my father had decided to return to the ruins of Warsaw and rebuild with others a life in his native land? Or if Iris and Richard had never met? My father with his charm and wit able to convince my mother of... something. And Iris, recovering from all she'd been through: three of her sisters killed during the war, a husband who had left their marriage for another woman, and the alcoholism that had already taken shape and would combine with other factors to take her life some thirty years later. What to say of what happened, what could have but didn't happen? My father at a certain moment chose from all the possible options available to him to come to London on a certain day and time, to begin working among fellow Poles in an émigré community that felt partly like home to him even in exile, one that many years later is still there, though now mixed with other populations who have settled there in that part of London, refugees from their own distant homelands: Pakistan, Senegal, Serbia.

And Iris? Who can say what she saw when she first met my father. She'd finished high school in Britain and had gone to work as a journalist when she was 19. Before the war she'd married a young man named John Laker. They'd been married for two years before he was called up, and when she said goodbye to him it was in the belief that their love was strong, and he'd return to her once the war was over. There were letters, yes, she'd said to me, there were some beautiful letters he wrote her from France, Italy, finally Germany after the Reich fell. And a silver bracelet that was inscribed with the initials of her married name—"IL"—that she'd worn until the end of her life, despite bitterness she never foreswore accompanied by a strong attachment to the man she had once married.

"He ended up being a shit," Iris told me one day. "A real shit." Apparently, John had been stationed in Wales when the war ended, where he'd taken up with a young Welsh woman. She got the news from his last letter sent to her in London. "The bastard was up there, and I was thinking all this time, how lovely when he comes back, you know, how wonderful it will be to have him again, and he hits me with this news. I was devastated, I can tell you, just fucking devastated." Then, after a pause, "He was the god's honest love of my life. I'm not lying, Andy, he was my first and only real love." I don't think I understood the impact of what she was saying at the time, didn't ask why, then, if John had been her one love she'd decided to marry again. Or what that made of Richard, with whom she'd shared her life since after the war.

My mother spent the 1940's writing for the *Edinburgh Current, London News Chronicle* and *March of Times and People,* political features and book reviews primarily. "IT MEANS WAR. says Iris Laker, who in this brilliant dispatch, exclusive to MARCH, throws light on the European scene." reads the banner headline of one of my mother's articles from March 24, 1948. Another headline, this one from March 31, 1948, reads: "1939 ATMOSPHERE IN EUROPE, Says Iris Laker, March's European correspondent. Did Stalin Anticipate U.S. Conscription? Finland 'Written Off'." These articles still exist in archives somewhere, perhaps digitized, perhaps not, perhaps only in piles of faded newsprint in the former offices of now-defunct news organizations—or, as in my case, in the boxes of materials I've saved from my parents' marriage.

What had drawn my father and mother together initially?

What were the circumstances of their first meeting? Mutual friends had introduced them at a party (or so I was told by my father), after which my father courted my mother for a period of several months before they decided to marry. Speaking little English, what could my father have said to Iris in those early days? Or she, with little knowledge of Polish, said to him? *Your father was a beautiful man when we met, he was a lovely gentleman, strong in his gaze, I recall that, I recall his way of putting the paper down on the table and extending his hand to me, very sweet, a small thing, but so much of what we knew came from such small things.*

A year following their meeting in London, Iris and Richard were married in a civil ceremony in London. I was told by a mutual friend of theirs that Richard wore the same Bond Street suit that day that he would wear a decade later when he and Iris traveled to New York to collect their newly adopted child. I have no way of confirming this, but like to think that for Richard the symbolism of that gesture would have been important, even if unarticulated at the time.

*

Richard's entries in the black notebooks he kept at the time during the period just before they would leave for America give one portrait of a relationship charged by such misunderstandings and conflicts. My father's clipped sentences in contrast to what he is reporting on. The "humiliating words" spoken by my mother in face of my father's "lost nerves." Something near to despair in my father's language even as it's as if he is away from himself when he writes of these experiences that have the sting of dashed hopes, the recognition of marital failing: *We were happy, we went away together, to Brighton, to the countryside. Iris was happy when we went away, then there would be quarrels, then the same and everything would be fine.* A pattern they both accepted—didn't accept—in different ways and to different degrees.

And what my father wrote so early in their marriage seems not to have changed greatly in all the years that followed, as if there had always been and always would be the "magnificence" of an evening destroyed by Iris's alcohol-infused anger:

> After having a tea in the H. of Cornwall bar we went to the embassy. We carried with us all the time the huge plate, a gift for us from K., which we decided to offer to R. We were invited to them the same evening. On our way to the embassy we had a big quarrel, then the same thing happened half an hour later when we went to the dentist. All was caused by my mistakes: we got out too late from the bus on our way to the Embassy. I forgot the address of the dentist. These were small things but Iris each time became furious like I really committed something very bad. I had to listen to very many humiliating words. I can tell today frankly that I have a big estimation for myself that during all this quarrels I never lost my nerves. After very nice evening with R., I had again a terrible return home ~~listening~~. She was furious that we stayed so long and of course it was my fault that the trains in London went too slowly, that in the evening they were not so frequent, etc. I was very miserable that she destroyed all the magnificence of that evening and that she could not understand that saying loudly to my best friends who were so close to us and to her as well so many bad things was very difficult for me. I was a little moved and wanted to stay with them longer.

Humiliation followed by remorse. Had my mother read these entries? It would seem so, as the numerous strikeouts and added words in my mother's hand would suggest that not only had she read them, she had been helping my father learn grammatical written English through these "exercises."

Iris and Richard traveled aboard the Queen Mary, leaving from Southampton, England, on March 22nd, 1949, a Thursday. In one photograph of my father from that time, he stands near a railing, the grey ocean just visible behind him. One arm resting on the railing, the other at his side, he looks straight into the camera, held by my mother. What does she see at that instant? His handsomeness? His love for her? Years later, sitting on our sofa in our house on Ordway

Street, my mother would point to this photograph in an album she kept in a bookcase near the fireplace, and say to me, "He was so lovely then, your father, so smart and beautiful, a man I couldn't have imagined meeting." Her eyes bore great tenderness for him at such moments. I can't say now which was more difficult: recognizing the softness with which she could still regard him, or realizing how muted and malformed their love had become in the years I spent with them.

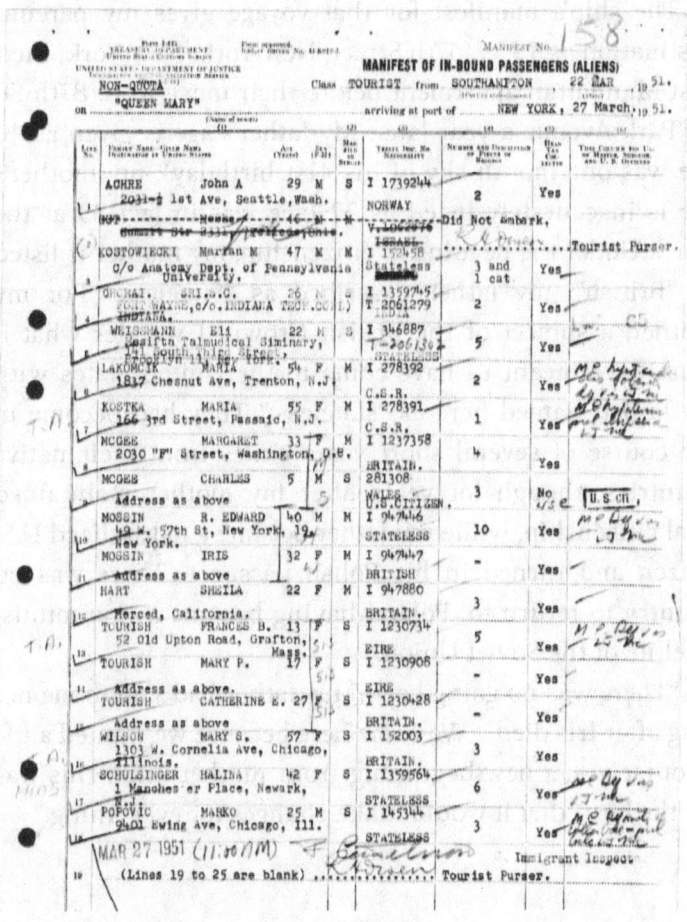

"Iris could be very kind," my father said to me once, "buying me small presents when I couldn't afford anything. A shirt, some ties, shoes when I needed them. She was very nice to me when I was a poor refugee, little English, no money, but she took good care of me." It was hard to believe, given what I saw, that this relationship was as he said. Though for my father, these were simple acts of kindness perhaps, enough for him to feel that he was, in fact, being taken care of.

The ship's manifest for that voyage gives my parents' destination as 49 W. 57th Street, New York, New York, their first Manhattan apartment before their move to E. 87th St. off Park Avenue a year later. My father's age is given as 40 (he was one month shy of his 41st birthday); my mother's age is inaccurately listed as 32 (she was in fact 33 at the time). Under the heading of citizenship, my mother is listed as "British"; my father described as "Stateless." For my mother, a subject of the British Crown, I wonder what it must have meant to have come to the United States with my father, named here as "stateless." They had become in the course of several short years exiles from their native countries, though for years after my mother maintained dual citizenship, while my father became a naturalized U.S. citizen and turned in his Polish passport. There was no country to return to, Poland having become a Communist satellite of the Soviet Union.

"There was no going back," my father had said to me not long after Iris died. "We came here because we wanted a life to ourselves, a new beginning. Your mother knew this was for the best, that it would make changes for everything."

In the same black notebook in which he'd described the early days of their marriage, Richard put down in some detail the journey to America he and Iris made together aboard the Queen Mary. The writing, surprisingly descriptive for my father, is filled with details meant to capture the scene, convey the mood of the trip. Mixed in with my father's typewritten text is my mother's hand, shifting tenses, underlining places for my father to return to. It's not clear for whom he was writing, though it seems to have been in part an element of my father's journalistic self to keep track of events, times and dates, record them so that they didn't get erased:

> I left England by Queen Mary just before Easter on March 22nd. The water was still rather chilly, although the first day of the spring had passed. There was rather still winter in the air. We went for last time for a walk at the beautiful Regent Park but the flowers and trees were completely barren from blossom. The Queen Mary garden was still flowerless. The journey to Southampton was quick, lost only one and half hour after passing all passport and custom formalities. We took our suitcases in our cabin prepared for the journey ahead. Queen Mary was to leave the next day in the morning so we have enough time to visit the beautiful big ship. She was built on....Each class several bars and restaurants, shops, pools and gymnasiums. Of course in the first class everything is even more luxurious and bigger. There is more room for the passenger to walk on the board. In the tourist class everything is more tight. But what the most amazing is that you can buy during your journey everything beginning from the chocolates and perfumes to the most luxurious dresses and suits and all much less than in the U.S. or in the U.K. The food is excellent and for all the passengers from England, it looked like from the other world. The program of the journey became from the first day very standardized.

After breakfast we used to play ping pong and sunbathe on the deck. The weather in that part of the year was not very sunny but rather windy, although it never rained. We spend the next part of the morning in the bar reading and drinking. After lunch the weather became generally better and then you could sit in the deck chair in the open air. After 4 or 5 when the first dark had fallen the passengers returned again to bar or play bingo and of course drank, as drinks were usual cheaper than on land. The captain organized several games to make the journey nicer: horse racings...But frankly speaking I think that this kind of journey must be very nice in summer time, because then you can take the deck chair and spend all day in the sun. In the winter and earlier spring when it still cold and you cannot be too long on the deck – your journey although lasting only 5 days becomes dull. The difference in time between London and New York is regulated in this way that every evening before going to bed the passengers turn their clocks back one hour. Owing to this you sleep every night one hour longer and after five days and night you have in you made the exact time.

What my father noticed—the activities, weather, the way time shifted—forming a world in a language that wasn't ever my father's own, situated between Polish and English, as if a continent separated him from his own world and the world he had come to recognize were always foreign, other, neither here nor there. There is the idiomatic awkwardness, the sense of a translation, of writing from a different tongue. It's occurred to me that for Richard, a non-native speaker and writer of English, the world he shared with my mother must have seemed very strange, difficult to understand, as if he too were one of those "dirty foreigners" my mother so often spoke of years later in America. And it explains as well some of my father's initial attachment to his Greek-born adopted son who struggled with words for many of the first years of his life and heard the world in phrases and words that always seemed in the process of being translated, of being given back to him in a new, more familiar tongue.

One afternoon Iris, in her early 40's at the time, two decades younger than I am now, said to me, "You can't change what happens to people when they meet, you can't change a thing, it's all there in the first minutes, first hours. When I met your father and knew it would be a life, something like a life we would live, no thought of children, of what could come, I knew we would come to this point, yes, to this and no other." She paused, inhaled as if to catch her breath, then continued. "But, Andrew, this kind of loneliness and lack of any care was made; it took time for us to make it. I knew that then...saw us on that path you could say...but it's because we didn't have a choice, we did and we didn't, that your father and I stayed together. It was too late even as it was just beginning."

Iris would say many such things to me over the years, confessions of a kind that formed a sort of bond between us, as if through listening to her I could enact with her that attitude of fatefulness and thwarted hope that I would hear the way children do: *These are the things of the world as they are, these are things that cannot be changed.* My mother's voice would trail off, the day would go into its next phase. I would return to my bedroom or stand on the porch outside while my mother remained sitting on the sofa where I'd just left her.

If I thought of my birth mother at all at those moments, I would have understood that another woman in another part of the world was keeping a different record, a different kind of faith. *Never be so far from yourself you can't find your way back,* she might have said, her voice in a near whisper as she leaned close into me. *Never go so far away you can't see the reason you came.*

One held faith as the object lesson of loss, the other as its steady arc toward life. In between, their child learned to read the world from the shattered pieces that remained.

SEVEN

When I was five years old in the fall of 1963, we moved to a house in Cleveland Park, just up the street from the Uptown Theatre and several blocks up from the National Zoo. I remember visiting the house with my parents before we owned it and lived there. After walking through the empty rooms of the first floor, sliding on the shiny newly polished oak plank floors, I headed down to the basement, moving into the dark, the stairway and steps down illuminated by light from the side door's window. Against the far wall, I discovered an old metal fold-up trundle bed left by the former owners of the house. Crawling between the layers of ticking, I hid myself there and listened from within the folds of the mattress while, above me, my parents walked through the rooms of the house where we would spend the next ten years together before my mother's death in 1971. The basement walls were unpainted limestone, with lines of moisture forming in the crevices. I lost track of time, folded myself deeper into the cave of the abandoned bed and listened for the sounds of them moving through the house, the voices of Iris and Richard collecting above me. And it was as if we had always been of this place together, this house not far from the one to which I'd been brought at a little over a year-old and that house shaped already by memories I had of a different landscape, a different house, a different country.

In time my mother came downstairs and searched the basement, turning on the light above the washing machine, creases of it creating a glow around her figure as she found me and pulled me out from my hiding place. Years later, my father would joke that perhaps I was waiting to be discovered by the original owners of the house so that I might become their child. I still have dreams in which I'm wandering through the rooms of this house, disguised, unnoticeable, sometimes accompanied by my mother, moving up into the first floor, up the stairs, through the darkness, away from the hiding space below. When we come to the top of the stairs we move out into the light again, and the back garden, awash in spring color, rises up in view like a wave of river water spilling over its banks. In other dreams, I see Iris working her way through the back garden, up past the newly flowering peonies and roses, her face burnished by sun light flowing to either side of her, creating a space for her, a furrowed crease of light moving across the world in which she lived.

*

I can't remember the first time Iris told me that I had been adopted, though as I recall it I was six or seven at the time—so this would be 1964 or '65. Perhaps it was a Friday in May, the wind sparse and uneven through the trees outside the window of our house on Ordway Street and the sun beginning to lose its light as we headed into evening. Perhaps it was summer and just past a full moon and she had come into my room and sat on my bed and told me the story of my adoption. Perhaps in an evening over chess, my mother's hand resting above a pawn as she planned out a strategy that would have her win the third of five games we would play that night, her voice nearing a whisper, then fading. *Yes,* she might have said, *what I'm telling you is true. Though nothing need come of it. You're here now, with us. You're our child.*

Whenever I was first told, over time the stories of my birth and my birth parents became cyclical, or the stories' telling became so through repetition, so that I could anticipate with each new telling what was coming next, Iris's voice shifting, the cadence moving into its customary rhythms as she spoke of the same "facts," the same enlarged story that was framed around a few simple things. The first, the second, the third times merged together, as if they were all part of one continuous narrative arc: beginning in the rape of my mother by my father, followed by pregnancy, his refusal to marry her, and ending with my adoption. The "facts" delivered each time with certainty, even as what Iris seemed to know and what was possible for her to know were separated in ways I wouldn't understand until years later. But those afternoons and nights when she spoke of the events surrounding my birth and adoption, I would most often stand before Iris in the center of the living room and she would be seated on the sofa underneath the gold leaf mirror that appeared in photos of their Manhattan apartment from the 1940's. On the table in front of her there would be gin or Scotch in a tall glass, her ashtray filling with each new cigarette she'd light up across the session. It's not inaccurate to call these "sessions," because they were exactly that, seemingly with no particular endpoint in mind, no way for me to exit or interrupt, my mother's voice falling across me like a long shadow that couldn't ever be entirely avoided. I would be told to stand, not to move, my body growing tired as the language came over me and I shifted my weight from right foot to left and back again, until it was an hour, then two, sometimes three, her voice catching on itself, collecting itself, starting over as need be.

"They were strangers, you mother and father," Iris might begin one of her accounts. "They were peasants who lived in the countryside, not far from Athens. One day your father approached your mother in an olive grove near her home and took her into the field where he raped her." She would pause, let the word, "rape," settle in before continuing. "When your mother became pregnant, your father, a soldier in the military, refused to help and abandoned her. Your mother apparently tried to get help from the local magistrate, but had no luck in forcing your father, Efthymios, to do anything for her." Iris would stop here, look at me as if appraising my ability to understand what she was telling me, then continue. "Your father wasn't a good man. A really selfish man, from what I have heard. Apparently he had another woman in the next town and it was with her he'd eventually have a family. As for your mother, well—" Iris would pause, take a deep breath for dramatic effect, then say, "It was very tough for her, a rape victim in that poor country at that time. No one wanted anything to do with her, so she traveled to Athens and gave birth to you in the children's hospital the Americans had built after the war. One of the best in Europe, or so we were told. When she left you in the orphanage attached to the hospital, one of the nurses later told us, your mother insisted that you be baptized in the Greek Orthodox faith, and so you were. Antonius. Anthony. Almost sounds like Andrew, doesn't it?"

In other re-tellings, Iris focused on the illegitimacy of my birth. "You were a bastard child," my mother would say, emphasizing the word "bastard," as if it were repulsive for her to say the word. "Bastard." The word hung there between us, repeated, even as I uncertain of its meaning. Once she spelled it out for me in Greek on a piece of paper near her nightstand: Μπάσταρδος. *Bastardosz.* I stared down at the Greek writing in my mother's hand, and saw a world come through, providing me with a context for my beginnings. Μπάσταρδος. My mother would hover near the word, insisting on its place in sentence after sentence, as if this single word were what she had to offer in place of other orienting facts. Bastardy in place of what else she could have—might have—said.

"You were a bastard," Iris repeated, "unwanted by either of them, that's why you were left in the hospital and even there no one really wanted a Greek baby so many months old already, no one."

There was sometimes a marble or toy soldier in my pajama pants pockets and I'd move my fingers around these objects while she talked. I often had the feeling that if I stood before her long enough, like rainwater in a slow moving downpour, the world would disappear in a torrent of water and our bodies with it. And I would imagine the woman and the man in these accounts, tasting the sea salt of a beach I'd never known, experiencing the light of a hillside I'd never seen. Sometimes after I'd been released from one such session, I'd lie on my bed and listen to the birds outside my window and invent the faces that had been brought to me: their eyes that were softened by age, their mouths that spoke in a tongue I couldn't recognize but that was at the same time familiar to me through the Polish I'd heard since I'd been an infant, as if Polish were a kind of Greek and

Greek another form of Polish, the words spilling across my skin darkened by the low forming clouds across the sky in Washington evenings that were filled with the scents of honeysuckle and magnolia.

The politics of Iris's love for me..... her absence coupled with that of another. At the ages I was, what could I know yet of these affirmations that were also erasures? *I am giving you your history so you can know who you are,* the woman said to me. *I'm bringing you close to your origins, as close as I can, to those who were so poor, they had nothing, nothing but you to give up.* The equation simple enough to understand, as if birth rite and economic poverty were co-equal, were the line drawn on a map of an island nation, my body brought across, re-situated, so that I could be told again: *There were these people, they are in your blood, there were these two...*

Their voices and mine, caught inside my head, a conversation that seemed to have no ending or beginning, the way the words mounted up, a lifetime of them, and I could see them taking me to the same place each time. "You were a bastard...your mother was raped," as if these were the formative, the only facts I needed to know.

I found myself standing one day in the living room when Iris came out of the kitchen, a freshly poured glass of amber liquor in her hand.

"Do you really know what the problem was?" my mother said, taking a seat on the sofa in front of me.

I stood inside a circle of light and sound, not moving one way or the other.

"Your father raped your mother. Yes, raped her. On a hill outside her home in that tiny village you're from."

My mother's face was calm, unimpassioned as she spoke. "She was a peasant," she continued, "and your father was a peasant too, neither had any education. What can you expect? This was the act of an ignorant man against an ignorant woman."

And how do you know these things? Who has told you?
They exist, they're part of your story. No one has told me.
So how can you believe them?
They are facts of these people, I cannot put it any other way. They are every part of what and who you are. All we can do is try to provide you something else, something better.
And if I am unable to change, to become that better son?

The estrangement was verbal, so I would sometimes be sure of only one thing: the kind of love I wanted would never exist here, in this world. The kind of love I wanted that was here maimed, mis-spoken, unseen.

Who brought you here? Who are you?

"I'm no one," I said. "No one at all."

EIGHT

There were rows of daffodils lining the hills of Rock Creek Park the spring of 1966 when I turned eight. I would see them in passing while sitting next to my father in our car as we headed to his office in Southeast where he would sometimes bring me for an afternoon. I would walk through the lime green corridors of the Human Services Building on 7th and D Streets, glancing out the big windows across downtown Washington, the broad avenues disappearing in the fading light of late afternoon or sometimes darkening, falling into night before we'd get back in the car and head home again.

Spring quickly advanced to summer, as I finished second grade. My father disappeared and returned to our house, sometimes gone for days, or so it seemed. I played a game while my mother cooked, making a knocking sound on the wall in the living room in imitation of his knock on the front door. When no one entered and the knocking continued, Iris would emerge in the middle of the hallway and look into the shadows gathering outside and glance over at me and wave her hand, as if to say, *Enough of that now.*

The days were porous, visible only by their beginnings and endings with light shifting, changing as the hours advanced, backward and forward it seemed to me, one could never say. My mother, softened by drink, would often sit on the sofa in the front room, a newspaper or book at her side, the glasses of clear and amber liquid arrayed on the glass table before her. It was how I often found her, afternoons, sometimes mid-morning, when I would come downstairs, Richard having left for the day or not having returned from the night previous or the night before that. It was a continuum, not an advancement of time, and I swam willingly in those open waters like a child moving into the waters of the sea and not turning to look back at how far from land he'd swum.

There was, that summer, day camp my mother sent me to, Beauvoir, part of the National Cathedral School. Each morning the bus would come up Ordway grinding its gears as it pulled to a stop in front of our house and when I left I'd turn once to watch the door close behind me, or stay open, depending on whether Iris had gotten up from her place on the sofa. Later in the day, having been dropped again in front of my house, I'd sometimes walk back up the hill toward Reno Road, then cross to the other side, moving toward Wisconsin Avenue in the mid-afternoon heat, no one around, no one to say anything to me or I to them. I would make my way past the early 20th century Victorian homes of Cleveland Park and imagine what it would be like to live in this one or that one, to wake up in a different house from the one I was returning to.

Stepping inside our house again after hours away I'd notice the pages of *The Washington Post* strewn on the floor next to the glass coffee table on which usually rested empty glasses, stained with drink. My mother would have gone upstairs and it would be evening or later before she would return.

Did I hear voices? Whose voices did I hear?

I'd begun talking to myself, walking home, in my own inner voice addressing myself, as if I were two people: two

Andrews, one worried that he was going crazy, that maybe there was something wrong with him, the other patient, holding him with one hand while they walked together.

Andrew, I'd say, hearing the words leave my mouth and enter the spring air as I walked toward school, *Andrew you're not crazy, you're not. Don't believe them! You're good kid, you're a good Andrew, you're not crazy.* Other times, Andrew would invent stories for me about things he imagined me doing. *Andrew, there's this place you're going to go one day, an amazing place with people who look just like you. And you'll wake up each morning to the scent of fig and oranges and the light will come through your window from the sea and you'll hear others with your voice talking to you, taking you inside again.* I didn't know what inside was or what it might look like, only that I lived with two selves: one the protector and the other one in need of protection.

As I got near home, Andrew would stop talking to me or I to him and I'd come back to the house and hear my mother in the kitchen preparing vegetables for lunch or the sound of her upstairs moving from room to room and I would know that this was my place, this was where I belonged.

Then it would come back to me and I'd understand all over again what was wrong. It didn't seem to matter what Andrew said. One Andrew believed he was crazy. I knew I was crazy. I thought I'd come this far, somebody would recognize what had happened, somebody would see there'd been this mistake. A mistake had been made. *I didn't belong. I don't belong. I'm not belonging.* Sitting at the top of the landing night after night, I'd stare down and hear Richard and Iris, and I'd hear myself lodged between them in fitful whispers and shouts and the voice was always the same in my head and it didn't match what they were saying and I didn't know how to make one stop and the other come forward.

Andrew, I said, *Do you think I'm crazy?*

And Andrew would always say the same thing, *Andrew, you're ok. They're the crazy ones. They're the ones who are screwed up, not you.*

But I didn't know how to say, "I'm not crazy, I'm not," and have them see.

My name wasn't my name. My life wasn't my life. I said these things to no one at all, said, "Take me back where I came from, I'm not crazy, I have a home where I belong," said to myself as I lay on my bed in the morning and later in the afternoon sun. Said to no one at all. No one to tell.

*

There were days when it all seemed okay: when my mother and father didn't seem to find fault, when I could be the boy they'd imagined having for a son, brought to live with them as if there had never been separation or the voyage out to get me. And at the same instant...I saw that they'd both reached the conclusion that something was wrong with me.

"The boy needs help," my mother would say, "There's something wrong.....He's not adjusting."

My father didn't say anything, his hands at his side, his eyes averted from both of us.

That fall I'd entered third grade at John Eaton Elementary but had already been placed in a special education classroom because of behavioral and language aptitude issues noted by the school principal. Apparently, I was still reading at a first grade level and there were concerns that I might not advance to third grade without significant assistance.

"I'll need to look at the district map again and see if we can't place you in a more accommodating school," the school principal, Mrs. Nickett, said to me one morning just after the first period bell had rung.

I stared at the map above her in the office where light seemed to come through the windows like light shot through celluloid and I'd imagined myself being taken to the far points of that map, east and west, north and south, being taken by train and left somewhere to fend for myself, wooded areas where at night you could hear the wolves in the mountains and the tall trees formed a dark perimeter....

I would get into fights often enough with other boys during recess and sometimes was sent home with notes from Mrs. Nickett, notes that I'd ask my mother to show me but she never would. One day after school I'd walked home with a boy in my grade who lived up the street from us, and something he said made me angry and we started fighting in the middle of Newark Street, heading down the hill toward home. We took our coats off and wrestled on the sidewalk until he fell onto the ground and I grabbed his coat and pushed it down into the sewer. He ran home after that and told his parents, who got in touch with mine, and my father said to me that we'd have to pay for a new coat.

"Why would you do such a thing, Andrew?" he asked me. "What is wrong with you?"

I didn't know what was wrong, only that I didn't want to be anywhere I was.

NINE

Days came and went. That fall I walked to school and back again, the leaves turning, the doors of houses painted the same beige and green they had been the fall prior. My mother was home most days and the afternoons used to seem like empty hours to fill before my father came home from work. Many nights he didn't come home until after I'd gone to bed, and I would hear him downstairs, in the kitchen, fixing himself a late dinner, as my mother remained behind her closed bedroom door.

What happened at school I can't remember except the smell of the hallways in the mornings when we first arrived, their ammonia-fresh scent that hit you when you first walked in the building. I was learning to read, not very well, and sometimes my mother would sit by me in the afternoons and try to have me pronounce the vowels and consonants as we were learning to do at school with the phonetic chart we read from each morning, a new vowel or consonant revealed to us every other day or so.

Some nights I went upstairs early, not long after dinner, and sat in my room before bedtime and listened for the birds that would come and rest in the uppermost branches of the oak whose branches hung like heavy black arms over our house. I would hear them downstairs, often arguing, sometimes the front door slamming, and I'd know that he'd left, and it wouldn't be clear to me those nights if he would ever come back, though in the morning again he would be downstairs, the radio going in his bathroom as he prepared for work.

What did I want? One night in the middle of one of my parents' fights I'd come downstairs and my father saw me standing in the doorway of our living room and I was wearing my pajamas and crying, though I couldn't say why. And my father said to me, "Andy, come to your tatuś, come to tatuś," using the Polish word for father, and I walked toward him as he sat in the heavy green armchair that rested by the front door, and he said, "Tell tatuś what's wrong, why you are crying?" and I was quiet, as I sat on his knee and my mother hovered nearby, seeming anxious or irritated by my presence, I couldn't tell.

I looked over at my mother, and said, "I just want you to stop fighting about everything." My father held me in his arms while my mother went into the kitchen and got something from the fridge, and I could hear the sound of liquid poured into a glass and she came back. The liquid in the glass shone like amber, as she put the glass down on the table and motioned to my father it was time for me to go back to bed. He gave me a kiss on the cheek and, as I passed my mother on the way out of the room, she glanced at me and seemed to smile, though I couldn't be sure.

Later, I heard them talking quietly but couldn't hear what they were saying, and as I drifted off to sleep, I realized that somewhere in the world were my *real* mother and father. I imagined that with them was the *real* Andrew, one who wasn't wrong, who did fit, whose mere existence didn't cause so many problems for those who had brought him here.

There were, during this time, weekly visits to Matthew Reynolds, a family psychologist who had his practice just across from the National Zoo in Woodley Park. I went at first with my father and mother together, then just with my father. The office had a play area with boxes of toys—Lego, Tinker Toys, small metal cars by Corgi and Matchbox—and I would be left alone at first when my parents went in to speak to Mr. Reynolds. When I was brought in, he would ask me questions about school, how the week was going, if there was anything I wanted to tell him. I would mostly stay silent during these sessions, and once in exasperation, my mother had turned to me and said, "Look, you need to help him so he can know what's wrong, why you're acting the way you are at home and at school." I saw something of a surprised look come over Mr. Reynolds's face and we had only a few more sessions with him before my father announced to me one evening in the late fall that I wouldn't need to go see Mr. Reynolds anymore.

"Why? Doesn't he like us?" I asked my father.

"No, nothing like this. He doesn't think there is anything more to do right now."

Years later, my father would tell me that Mr. Reynolds had concluded that I wasn't the one who needed the therapy but Iris, something that couldn't be expressed to her at the time. Until the end of her life, Iris tended to view psychology and psychologists as little more than palliatives, meant for the short term, possibly useful but not to be trusted overall. Yet she'd turned with my father to psychiatrists to find out what was wrong with their adopted son. She wanted to "root out the problem," she said to me once, to see if there was something wrong with my brain, perhaps something needed to be given me, she didn't know what, perhaps some medicine would help.

It was around this time that my mother started putting

something in my milk. The taste was chalky, bitter, I couldn't know from what. When I asked her, my mother took a sip from the carton and said, "Tastes fine to me."

I started falling asleep at school, putting my head down on the desk during morning classes, unable to get up when the teachers would come and shake me and I'd find myself in a circle of light from the high windows and feel the hands of Miss Alexander, my second grade teacher, on me and get up and move from my desk chair and slide it back under and be taken to the nurse's office. Once there, I'd climb onto the small bed they kept in the back of the office and sleep through the rest of the morning.

When I returned home in the afternoon, I would tell my mother I'd fallen asleep again at school: I thought there was something in the milk, it tasted weird. "Oh, Andy," she'd say. "Don't be ridiculous. The milk is fine. You're just spending too much time listening to us at night. Little eavesdropper." As if, I thought, she means *Stop mistrusting me, stop looking for things when they're not there.*

She put the kitchen towel back on the rack and walked into the dining room, where the light was changing yellow to orange, while outside our neighbor had started mowing his lawn again. The sound of the blades seemed to follow me as I wandered back out onto the porch out back and held onto the top of the laundry line, pulling it toward me so that it circled back out on the silver wheel attached to the house. The sound of the blades stopped, and our neighbor came around to the back of the house and pushed the mower underneath their porch and caught my eye as he turned and smiled toward me, then disappeared from view as he made his way back to the front of his house.

A few nights later, after my mother had gone into her room, I made my way soundlessly down to the kitchen and poured out the carton of milk into the sink. I would drink only water for a long time after that, no matter how many times my mother offered me a fresh glass of milk.

TEN

A month after our last session with Mr. Reynolds on a blistering cold January morning, my father took me for clinical psychiatric observation to the Children's Hospital of the District of Columbia. I was placed under the care of a psychiatrist, Dr. Hoffman, from January 9th through the evening of January 14th, when I was discharged at 7:15 p.m. The discharge papers from my stay list "Behavior Problem" as the final diagnosis. In the days leading up to my time at the clinic, my mother explained to me that I was being taken to a clinic for children and that it was only to determine that everything was all right with me. We were walking up the hill back home, bags of groceries pulled along in the shopping cart used in those years for trips to the Safeway on Connecticut Avenue.

"Will there be other children?" I asked.

"Yes, there will be other children just like you."

"*What are children like me?" I want to ask but don't.*

"What will they do to me?"

"They will see if anything is wrong with you." *Like something overheard from another room so that I took "wrong" into my mouth and let it rest there: "wronged," "wrung," "ring," kept spilling the words over and over like seeds pressed under my tongue.* "There'll be tests, I can't say what kind, just to make sure you are all right."

"Do you think something is wrong with me?" I asked, watching my mother's face for her response.

"I don't know," she said, readjusting her grip on the cart.

"Why am I going if you don't think something is wrong

with me?" My mother looked away, as if tasting something bitter, then glanced back down at me.

"We can't know for sure unless tests are done."

"What kind of tests?"

"Oh for god's sake," my mother said. "I don't know. Tests for your head, tests to make sure everything is as it should be."

Her hand moved as she spoke, as if brushing away flies, then settled back at her side.

"Will they hurt?"

"I don't think so, dear. It will likely last a few days then be done."

I held a book of short stories in my hand, given me by one of my teachers at school. The words made no sense to me as I listened to my mother and held the book open in the light and saw that silver had reversed and become "sliver."

"Can I come home each night?"

"No, dear, you'll be staying there every night."

"For how long?"

"We don't know yet, probably not more than four or five days."

"Will you come with me and stay with me?"

My mother looked straight up the hill as we approached 29th Street, then let the cart rest for a moment, while considering how to respond.

"I have to stay at home. Your father will come and see you, though."

I thought I heard her say "I have to come home," and I wondered what home was like when I wasn't there, how it would be different, what the days would look like with me gone, days they'd have to themselves, some part of my room coming into view even as she said it, so that home and room appeared as names for different things. I lived in a room not a home, they were living in a home, not a room. There was something in my mother's tone, something I heard as reluctance to be honest with me, as if she wanted to say but wouldn't. *We can't return you to where you came from, can't give you back, this is the best we can do.* And turning to go up the stairs with her that day, I noticed for the first time the heaviness in my mother's walk, the way her boots struck the pavement with this weight, this hardness, as if she was barely able to pick her feet up, as if they would stop one day, just stop, and her steps would freeze in place like wood that's fallen from the sky and doesn't shift from its place on the ground.

The next day, my father brought me in the late afternoon to the admissions desk and I was taken to Ward M-4, Room 411. After a few minutes my father left, and I was standing alone in the room and asked by a nurse wearing a white and blue name tag, "Julie" printed on it, to change into the hospital gown that had been left for me on the bed. I heard my mother's voice in my head telling me again, "We don't know for how long, we hope not long, you will have people to care for you."

I got under the sheets and waited for the nurse to come back, and when she didn't, I stared out the window and saw that the sky had shifted to a cobalt blue, and it was like the world was going to sleep, everyone in it was going to sleep, and I felt the first signs of nausea brought on by fear. *Andrew, I said, it's ok, it's ok to be here without anyone, you won't be left here for good.* And when the nurse came back and saw that

I'd been crying, she put her hand on my forehead and felt it and said, "You need some rest, child. Let's get you under those covers." I watched as her hands moved across the bed sheet and pulled the hospital blanket up around my chin, and I smiled at her as she patted me on the head and said, "It's ok, you'll be just fine here. Everyone's going to take care of you, don't you worry." She turned and left the room, so that I could see into the hallway the other nurses gathered at the station and their bodies were moving in slow motion, just the way dancers do across a stage.

The days came and went, I can't remember how the hours were spent, though I recall there was a group therapy session with other kids my age, once a day in the morning. We sat in a circle and talked to each other, as the young psychologist sat at the top of the circle and listened, not saying very much, occasionally adding positive reinforcement to someone's comment, but rarely more than that. Her face is beyond recall now, only the way her hands moved among the folders that sat on her lap, carefully organizing them as we spoke, and the tone of her voice, like licorice, so that you could almost taste the words as they came out of her mouth.

One day, another boy, Charles, was assigned to my room. He was older, maybe 12 or 13, there for psychiatric observation as well. His hair was cut in a page-boy cut, and he wore an earring in his left ear. Once I asked him about it, and he said, "Yeah, my dad didn't want me to get it, said it made me look queer. I told him what difference does it make; I like the way it looks," and he shrugged and looked over at me as if to see if I had any judgments to make as well. I put my hands in my lap and just stared back at him, having nothing to say in response.

Charles told me his mother had gone into a rehab clinic for a drinking problem, had been in and out of treatment, but this time she wasn't coming out for awhile, or at least that's what he'd heard, and now lived with his aunt and her boyfriend in an apartment building in southeast Washington. They'd been there for about a year when Charles started getting into trouble: fights at school, days he would cut all his classes and be found by D.C. cops who caught him loitering outside of stores in Adams Morgan, other parts of the city he'd go to, never sure where he was going, just that he wasn't going to do what he should be doing and stay in school. I asked him what it was like not being with his mom.

"Nothing special," he said. "It's not like she was around much to begin with."

"Same here," I replied, even as I knew that it wasn't true.

"Yeah," he said, "I don't know why but I don't miss her that much, just too hard to think on it, you know?"

He was working his way through a bag of potato chips and grinned at me and said, "You know what, god's honest truth?"

"What's that?"

"She'd be better off dead."

"You don't mean that," I said.

"Yeah, I do. Her life's been mess since day one, then I came along, and, well, it didn't get any better. Think she'd be happier gone. Really." Charles's face had this look of pained recognition about it, but that passed, and he was quickly joking again. "Shit, I may as well be dead too, better than being in here for this crazy show."

"I dunno," I said, "I don't really get why I'm here either."

We agreed we'd keep things straight between us, should

either of us ever need some reality check on what was happening to us. Meantime, we saw that whatever was being done was happening in a world that was soon enough going to put us back where we came from, no matter what else was found wrong with us.

In the afternoons, we played checkers and Parcheesi together in the sun room, and he would laugh out loud suddenly sometimes for no reason and put his hand on mine and suggest we do something together.

"Like what?" I'd say.

"I dunno, something." His mouth opened into a half-grin and I could see that two of his front teeth were missing.

"You mean something bad." I was sitting on one of the plastic fold-up chairs that had been left from a therapy session and, as he talked, light shone through the windows, dull and pallid, like a slow moving wave that pulled us inside it.

"I dunno. Maybe."

"Like what?"

"We could run away."

"Where to?" I said, as I remembered what it had been like when I'd run away from home before, which was part of the reason I'd been brought in for observation. "Out of control," my mother had said, "completely out of control." *What of it?* I'd thought at the time.

ELEVEN

I thought I understood Charles, got what it was that drove him, just as I'd understood long ago that there wasn't really any one place for kids like us. Running away was what we did, what we knew. And as Charles continued talking, making up some new scheme for us to get away from the hospital, I was remembering the night the previous summer when I'd snuck out after my mother and father had gone to sleep and walked up the alley to the house of a family we knew from the neighborhood. I didn't have any idea where I was going or what I'd do once I got there. When I came to the top of the alley, I looked back down and there was this darkness settling over the streets, as if shadow and light made this fog covering the world, so that everything lost shape and depth. I kept moving up the alley into the next block and found my way to the house of a kid I'd sometimes played with after school. His folks had a storage box on their back porch with a lid that opened from the outside, while the other half of the chest jutted into their bedroom. I lifted the lid and climbed in and smelled the mothballs and soaked canvas of the interior of the box seat and fell asleep on the slightly moist cushion that lined the bottom of it.

At some point in the night I woke and bumped my head against the top of the storage chest, half of which jutted into their bedroom through the separating wall. From inside the house, I heard a man's voice yell to stop and get out, then the sound of the door to their bedroom opening as he came out onto the porch and pulled the lid open. The stars were bright black green above him in the trees and he held out his hand and said, "What the—" Then he gave me his hand and pulled me out.

From inside, I heard my friend's mother calling my parents and saying, "Yes, he's here, seems he was sleeping in our storage box, yes, yes, oh I don't know how—Sure, we'll make sure he doesn't go anywhere."

When I stood in the light of their bedroom, I could still feel the night air sharp and cool around my ankles and legs bare without trousers and I let them look at me without saying a word until my father arrived. He was wearing his housecoat over pajama bottoms and t-shirt and he apologized to them and thanked them for not calling the police and took me down the stairs out the back way into the alley and he pushed me down the hill where he said my mother was waiting for me for answers. When we came in, she was sitting on the sofa, a cigarette burning in the ashtray and a drink in her hand.

"Well?" she said.

"Iris," my father said, "let the boy go to bed."

"Nothing to say?"

I walked toward the stairs and heard her gulp down the rest of her drink.

"Fine, fucking fine," she shouted after me, as I went up the stairs, while in the kitchen my father was putting water in the kettle.

Upstairs in my room the light was changing, low orange opening into cool bands of early morning light. The sky seemed like a perimeter, a border between this world and the next. When I lay my head on the pillow the birds had gone quiet, the trees without sound, as if each branch were a strip of black tape across the light and your hands could trace each one from end to end, the branches meeting then separating, pulled apart by the low forming weight of color on a sharply detailed border.

*

Charles was still talking, still going on about his plan for us. "We could go to Baltimore, I've got friends we could stay with."

"What about your aunt?" I asked.

"She doesn't have to know."

"How would we get there?" I said. Charles made a motion with his thumb.

"Walk?"

"Nah, hitch."

"You think we could? Isn't it far?"

"Not that far."

I looked out the window and saw the sun setting now over Michigan Avenue and heard the roaring of the buses passing below.

"You're funny," I said.

"You think so?"

"Yeah." He leaned over and opened his gown, and I saw the curling blond hairs of his pubis and looked away.

I looked out the window again instead and saw that it had gotten dark out and the lights were on in the office building opposite us and in the hallway a nurse was making rounds, offering dessert of Jello and ice cream. I got off the bed and stood by the window and waited for the lights to go out as they would, one by one, and Charles disappeared into the hallway. I don't remember if he came back or if he left our room that evening, never to return. Somehow, it seemed at the time appropriate that he should have gone as he did, and later I would find out from one of the nurses that Charles had gotten as far as the end of the block when they caught him, still wearing his hospital gown and slippers, and brought him back to the ward.

TWELVE

An EEG was done early one morning. The doctor who performed the procedure comes back to me now as delicate-boned, with short blonde hair like that of a girl who lived down the street from me. I recall looking up at him as he applied the alcohol-scented gel to my scalp and watching his fingers move through the different colored wires that he attached to small plastic cups, before also placing these on my scalp. The smell of alcohol was overwhelming, and I started to cry, and he said, "Don't worry it'll be over soon," and then there was the sound of the machine near the wall and his hands were making movements in the dark room. I couldn't see him, he'd disappeared from view, then come back and his fingers adjusted the dials again and the smell nearly made me sick, and he leaned over as if to kiss me on the cheek and said, "Just a little more it'll be done in a minute just hang on," and I did hang on until he stopped and had disconnected the electrodes and pulled the screen back from the door and turned the lights on. He came over to me and helped me into a wheelchair, and I was taken back to my room.

Charles was already gone, and the light was short and sharp across the linoleum when a woman I didn't know came in and got the last of Charles's belongings, and I sat down on the bed by the empty wheelchair and waited for something else to happen.

Yet what had happened I couldn't recall. Even when the night time came it was as if the surface of the earth were covered in red gauze and the filters were gone and nothing could be seen for as far as eyes could see and I remembered a book my mother had read me once about the young prince who escaped his planet by taking advantage of a migration of wild birds and on the morning of his departure he had sought to put his planet in order, the red with the green, the blue with the black. He had come to a sea of lava and sat beside it and saw the fleck of embers burning hot and bright in the sand and he carefully raked the volcano ash until it became warm underneath the soles of his feet. He traveled like that, uprooted, exiled, traveled away farther still until he came to the edge of another ocean and there were geese nearby and a fountain of red sky and he lay near each pillar that rose like a funnel out of the clay. He poured water over his flesh and waited until the time that his flowers would bloom and, nearing the edge of the grey green sea, he lay near the tallest flower, brittle and spiky in its bloom, took to it some soil and took away from it some light until he and the flower were one part of the scene and the world beyond them lay nearly incomplete, nearly imperceptible, as water and light flowered together in one place.

My father came to visit in the evenings and brought me Matchbox cars from the gift shop in the lobby and sometimes chocolates. He would come around 6:30 and stay until visiting hours ended at 8 p.m., but most of the time he would wander the halls, spending perhaps 20 minutes in the room with me. I don't know where he went, though as I waited for him to return I would imagine him roaming the halls, peering into other children's rooms, as if looking for one he had lost. When he returned he might speak to me affectionately in Polish, as if I could understand, had been taught to understand. *Rozumiesz mnie wiesz, co mam na myśli?* Do you understand? Do you know what I mean? Leaning down over my bed in the hospital, he would speak words that came like that, without translation, "Andy, everything will be fine, don't worry, you will go home soon."

Drifting off to sleep those nights, long after he'd left, I would still hear him through the night speaking to me as if I were truly one of his own, of his own blood, as perhaps his father had spoken to him. And I thought how strange to be here in this world where his father isn't and his own people aren't and yet there are the three of us like this resting together as if in some unnamed region of the world, some place without name or nation state attached to it.

"Andy, be a good boy, sleep, don't worry what will happen," the voice at once melodic and jarring, as if coming from another world.

Once he appeared with flowers that had been left in another room after the patient had left, and he offered them to me, beginning in Polish, saying, "Andy, look, some pretty flowers for your room, the same that Iris would like." The bouquet included six roses, baby's breath and six pink carnations, and had been placed in one of those FDS faux crystal vases with the neck that tapered up to a small mouth. For the next three nights of my stay I kept the vase close to my bed, and watched as light from the TV flickered around it in arc-like waves and listened to his voice made from phrases I didn't understand but knew as the language of home.

The week passed and I was taken back to Ordway Street and my mother made eggs and bacon for me the first day I was back and said, "Andy, you were such a good boy with all those awful tests, it must have been terrible, but now you're home we can spend the days together again." I didn't know how to react to my mother's sweetness, never did, knowing well what so easily and quickly could follow it. I stood at the edge of our living room and listened to the sounds from outside.

My father stood out in the snow with his shovel and the alleyway was covered in the new snowfall and the streets around our house lay covered as well, and after breakfast I told my mother about Charles, and she said he sounded like a horrible American and I should stay away from American children, they were a bad influence. Then she petted me on the head and stroked my temples as I had been taught to do for her when she had bad headaches and she asked what I wanted to do today.

I said, "Go play in the snow."

She smiled and went upstairs. I don't remember how long it was before she came back downstairs, though I turned every so often to see if she'd appear in the window to the den downstairs. When her face finally did appear, just for a second, it was like a ghost figure falling into place in the high wire light of early afternoon.

My father had removed himself from the house by the time I returned from sledding later that afternoon and for dinner I remember sitting downstairs and waiting for my mother to come down and going upstairs and finding her in bed, the covers pulled up around her face, and I went back downstairs and into the kitchen and found some mince meat pie still left from the night before. I sat at the aluminum table and forked out pieces directly from the tin pie plate and went to the window and watched the snow start falling again through the leafless trees.

THIRTEEN

Some of Dr. Hoffman's report from my stay at the hospital is unreadable now, whole sentences of his handwriting remaining indecipherable. I read his words several times when I first got the reports in 1993 from the D.C. Children's Hospital archive and each time another word that had at first been unreadable would become translatable, then would seem as if of its own accord to become a different word and I would start at the beginning of the sentence again.

Allergy with hyperactive organic brain syndrome

Final Diagnosis: Behavior Problem

7 ½ year old white male. Adopted son of this couple from Greece at age 13 mos. Nothing known about real parents or birth history. Has lived in hospital of birth til time of adoption. Admitted for workup of hyperactivity both at school and at home and poor attention span. This was first noted when he started kindergarten at 5 ½ years of age. He was described as teasing other children, disturbing class. However, he has been doing satisfactory academic work. Was watched a year ago by school psychologist. IQ seemed all right and described him as "unfocused." Since start of this year he has been in special class for social adjustments.

Strong social history – mother is known alcoholic and would have episodes of sadistic tendency, often punishing the boy or sending him out of the house, no food. Verbally admits that she cannot love him. Father seemed to try to be close to him but presently refused to intervene when mother goes into a bad mood because she becomes a "worse mother" to him and went into "bad mood yesterday" which prompted admission today.

>Mother – 46 years old – born in England.
>Father – 56 years old – born in Poland – working USIA.

Andrew was adopted at 13 mos., born in Greece, through International Social Service, product of illegitimate pregnancy, nothing known of parents. At 13 mos. was already crawling, attempted footsteps. Considered – normal – but very active.

Lives in house – 3 bedrooms – mother stays at home – father working 5 days a week. Mother drinks since their marriage, quite eager to have a child. Frequent coughing especially at night, more pronounced when excited.

Andrew lies to mother, rather often she is incensed by his duality, lying, stealing and other anti-social activities. The father would like to affect a separation between the two with a placement of Andrew outside of the house. The neurological examination of Andrew yesterday and today revealed a very hyperactive youngster who appears often quite exasperated, very anxious and most unpredictable. He is very verbal with fluxing changeable attitudes, patterns of interpersonal reaction. For instance yesterday he was rather indifferent to my presence and was significantly resistant to my exam. Today, however (perhaps because mother was present) he ran down the hall and made a significant display of affection, saying, "Here's Doctor Hoffman, my favorite doctor..."

Perhaps all of it happened as Dr. Hoffman said it did. Or perhaps, as I so often did in those days, I played the part expected of me, giving Dr. Hoffman something to put in a report I knew my mother would read, letting her hear him tell her that I lied, stole, was anti-social. It was as if I had given my life away, pled for another's to take my place. And so he had.

Later that spring, three months after returning from the hospital, I was sitting in the principal's office at John Eaton, watching Mrs. Nickett as she glanced over at her district school map. She was wearing a blue wool suit I had seen her wear many mornings already and her pince-nez glasses that leave an imprint on her nose when she took them off. On her desk there was a fresh cup of hot tea and a small vase holding fresh cut flowers from her garden.

"Now, what we want, Andy," she began, "what I'm afraid is very clear from what's been happening is that we need a new school for you." She looked down her glasses at me and her eyes were grey and still like bird's eyes.

I looked away, then up at her, and said, "Yes, ma'am."

She turned a page over from her roll book and scanned down the roster for Mrs. Alexander's class, whose homeroom I attended three days a week, and she hummed to herself while I sat before the window open onto the playground below, until finally Mrs. Nickett rose from her chair and pointed to a school that is about a mile away.

"This might work for you, but I'll have to see if there's room, they've had some new children moving in." She turned toward me and her mouth broke into a half smile, as she put her pointer down.

"You want to tell me what's been going on, Andy?"

"Nothing, ma'am."

"Nothing?"

"No, ma'am," I said, remembering my mother's words to me, "Others don't need to know our business, you don't want to wash our dirty linen in public."

"Anything going on at home?"

"No, ma'am, everything's fine."

"Hmmm," she murmured, crinkling her brow. "You pushed those patrol boys down the steps last week and the week before that you were caught stealing from one of the other children in your class and the week before that you were truant two days in a row. You sure everything's fine?"

"Yes, ma'am," I said. Outside I heard the first recess period about to end, the sounds of kids running up the back steps and into the hallway, while on the playground the kick ball hit the back of the fence and bounced on the asphalt.

"Well, okay then. You leave me no choice. Let's see how the rest of the year goes, but it looks like we'll need a new school for you by fall."

"Yes, ma'am."

She opened the door and gave me a weak smile as I got up and walked into the hall and returned to my classroom. I'd spent my entire recess in Mrs. Nickett's office and now the second recess period had begun and from outside I could hear the screams of the other kids playing kick ball and jump rope. I sat down in my chair in the empty room and noticed that Mrs. Alexander had left her marking pen on the desk and I got up and went over and held it in my hand, then put it in my pocket and returned to my desk. When I got home I placed the pen in my favorite shoebox that held all my special pens and Matchbox cars and Batman cards. Several months later, while cleaning the house, my mother found my box and said she was confiscating it, since everything in it had been stolen. I didn't tell her otherwise, but let her remove my box, knowing that one day it would come back to me, as all things eventually did.

During one of my last sessions with Dr. Hoffman before I was released from the hospital, he asked me to draw a picture of a man and woman with pencil and crayon. According to his notes, I was resistant at first, then drew a square-like torso, rounded shoulders and curling arms and upper body that was discernible and thicker than the lower portion. For the head I drew a protrusion with eyes and mouth. One leg was attached to the body, with the other and seemingly replaced by a cane because, as I apparently told Dr. Hoffman, "The man has lost a leg!" My drawing of a woman was similar, except for the absence of a cane and the presence of a yellow band drawn like the foundation of house for the woman's dress. The woman's hands were missing, as was her nose, and for eyes I had drawn two large black circles with green dots for pupils.

"Is she frightening to you?" Dr. Hoffman asked me.

"No, she's my mommy," I'd replied.

"And how about your dad?"

I thought about it for a moment and said, "He's harder to draw, he has a lot of stuff inside him that's hard to draw."

When I'd completed the drawings I handed them back to Dr. Hoffman and saw that his calendar was a month behind. On the bookshelf were photographs of what I assumed was his family, two sons and his wife. Their bodies were positioned in such a way that it was as if the photographer had wanted to create the impression that they were all looking just off to the side, so that their faces appeared in profile in a row. What were they looking at? I wondered as I sat in the office opposite Dr. Hoffman and listened to the whirring of the clock gears from the desk clock that faced away from me. I stared at the photograph for a long time while the doctor reviewed my drawings, taking notes as he did so, not once looking up from the pages on which I'd scribbled at the bottom in uneven block type my name, "Andrew."

Dr. Hoffman took my page of drawings and put them in a folder on his desk and led me back into the hallway, where one of the nurses took me back to my room. I wondered if Dr. Hoffman would show the drawings to my mother and father, but knew it wouldn't matter if he did. They were just pictures, like the ones I drew for school that my mother had taped to the walls of my bedroom.

FOURTEEN

The days after I returned from the hospital that spring were ones when nothing seemed to happen, as if the hours couldn't possibly pass any more slowly. Iris had asked me at first how I was feeling, if I'd felt any change from my time at the hospital, if the therapy group had made a difference. I didn't know what to say, mostly said nothing at all. I finished the school year as it had begun, uncertain of where Iris and Richard would put me next, where I would be taken, what the world would look like when I was moved to some new location again.

With June heat in D.C. on the rise, I was waking up to the sounds of the birds in the trees, the light streaming into my bedroom through the trees and creating oblong patches on the wall nearest the door. The house was still and quiet as if no one lived there. Summer seemed to come without warning, suddenly heating up the atmosphere in a blaze of humidity and scorching sun. The magnolia blossoms fell to the pavement after a heavy thunderstorm and the alley became clear again of their leaves. The roses came into full bloom underneath the windows of the den and, in the garden patch that my mother and I had planted with rows of marigolds, the flowers came into full bloom, row upon row of oranges and reds so that your eyes almost hurt looking at them.

On a sweltering August morning a little over three months after my stay in Children's Hospital, my father took me to live with a family who ran a small boarding school on a property known as Wild Goose Farm in Shepherdstown,

West Virginia. There was talk at first of a boarding school on the Chesapeake, then possible relocation to another foster family for a time, until finally Wild Goose Farm ended up being the alternative. After much searching and debate between my parents, my mother found an ad in *The Washington Post* for a boarding school in West Virginia. She showed me the ad one day in the spring and I didn't think much of it, just stared at it until my mother took it away from me and put it back in the drawer of the escritoire. A few weeks later, my father told me that we would be visiting the farm in June, just to see. He said it might be necessary to give my mother some rest for her "bad nerves." I knew what he meant, though didn't see the point in his lying to me about what was really going on.

My father suggested we visit before committing to the farm, so on a Saturday in June we made the drive from Washington to Shepherdstown. I later learned that Wild Goose Farm had been built in the 1830's as a plantation house with a row of icehouses in the back and two buildings for curing meat, all of them built by West Virginia stone masons more than a quarter century before the beginning of the Civil War. The farm had been designed by Richard Shepherd, the grandson of William Shepherd, the founder of Shepherdstown. As described by F. Vernon Aler who wrote a book on the history of Berkeley County, West Virginia and visited Wild Goose Farm in the 1880's, the property was meant to communicate a distinct, pastoral innocence and gentry-like charm: "Passing up a long avenue of well grown and carefully selected forest trees—beech, linden, maple, and others—we approach the mansion. Here on a knoll, embowered 'mid a profusion of waving willows, stately poplars, and quaking aspens, stands the residence, built in a quadrangular shape, with two extended wings – a pretentious frame structure of a comparatively modern architecture…We enter through a Gothic porch, a spacious hall, leading to the parlors, which are simply but richly furnished—skillfully reflecting mirrors and choice paintings adding to the pleasing effect."

The property we first saw that day hardly resembled Aler's description, though a few geese could still be spotted roaming near the pond in front of the main house and two horses paced together in the pasture that could be seen from the front porch of the house. The house itself had fallen into disrepair over the years, the front balcony showing its age, a few of the front railings missing and the paint on the wood paneled siding having cracked and splintered so that it was brittle to the touch and came off in my hands when I pulled off a piece as we were walking alongside the east-facing portion of the house. Even the paving shale that led up to the main entryway had chipped, each one having cracked into two or three separate pieces that rested like small grey islands in the moist soil.

Yet the farm, for all its broken-down aspect, still had a strangely compelling quality in the late spring light as my father and I walked around the property for a few hours and spoke to Mr. and Mrs. Ross, who were caretakers of the farm for the Captertons, the family who had owned Wild Goose since the 1940's. Most of the other boys had already left for the summer break at that point, though we were introduced to the Ross's sons, Matt and Evan, and an older boy, Jordan, who had been sitting on a tractor by himself as we walked across the front yard past the pond.

"Why don't you come over and meet our guests?" Mrs. Ross called out to Jordan. I watched as he got down from the tractor and climbed over the fence and made his way over to us. He was tall with a military-style crew cut, dungarees, a stained t-shirt, and shoes that looked like they didn't fit.

"Nice to meet you," he said, glancing sideways, and held out his hand to my father first, who shook it awkwardly, then to me. His palm was rough over mine and he had a small scar just above his ring finger that he later told me came from baling wire.

"Andrew's coming to stay with us in the fall," Mrs. Ross said.

Jordan looked over at the tractor and played with a piece of wood about the length of his hand. "That's nice," he said, then to Mrs. Ross, "Ma'am, I'd like to go back to work, if you don't mind," and she shrugged and said, "As you will, but don't forget we're having supper early tonight," and Jordan nodded toward my father and me and walked back toward the pasture and climbed over the fence and made his way through the hay bales that had already been piled up in one corner of the field.

As my father and I roamed the property that day, I remember feeling some odd kinship for the place, as if it proposed an alternative home space to the one I would be leaving. And at the same time, walking past the chicken coops and horse stalls, I somehow understood as I hadn't before what my mother meant when she had told me one afternoon that I'd be living on a farm in West Virginia for awhile to learn "what hard work really looks like." When was I coming back? My mother looked off that day and didn't offer anything conclusive. "Just a few months, maybe longer," she'd said, her hands resting on a tea towel in the kitchen.

We left to drive back to Washington late that afternoon and my father said, "It seems good, don't you think so?" and I looked out into the still bright June day as we passed a truck-stop selling beer and cigarettes for 75 cents a pack and said, "Yeah, I guess." My father and I didn't speak for much of the rest of the car ride home. When we got back it was past dinner time and the house was quiet and I went up to bed without supper, while downstairs I heard my father banging a pot on the stove as he prepared his dinner of frankfurters and beans.

FIFTEEN

By the time I returned to Wild Goose Farm in August, there would be seven of us, all boys: two, Matt and Evan, the sons of Mr. and Mrs. Ross; Jordan, whom I'd already met; and the other three from families living in D.C., Virginia, Maryland. I was given to understand that the reason we were at the farm in the first place was that we were all "troubled" in one way or another. It was mostly a quietly received understanding we shared with one another, as if we'd been brought together for this one purpose, to become somehow other than what we were: a group of boys whose families couldn't or wouldn't keep us anymore. *Here's the only place you've got, it's home, like it or not.* I don't know if I viewed this period as punishment or welcome escape from the home I shared with my parents. Probably a little of both. It was as if my mother were saying to me *You are living on borrowed time, you have only so many more chances to prove yourself worthy of our love before we give you up give up altogether and that will be the end of what we have to give, the end of our love.* At least that's what I heard in my head, her voice softly accusatory and oddly comforting at the same time.

In my recollection of those days it's the shades of turquoise that come to me most often. The wind moving through the open balcony window from the Ross's bedroom and the smell of eggs, bacon, and grits that permeated the entire house each morning. In the afternoons after school (we were taught by a 30ish teacher who showed up to work each morning in a bow tie and neatly pressed slacks and whose favorite book was Thor Heyerdahl's *Kon-Tiki*), I rode down the mile-long driveway on the post office bike I'd been given, then back up to the area to the side of the house where Mr. and Mrs. Ross parked their cars. I would ride in a circle, counter-clockwise, clockwise, counter-clockwise, clockwise, steering nowhere, moving in one direction then another, and as I rode I'd hear the hens in the chicken coop and Joe, the Ross's cook, calling out to us to come in for supper, and then the squalling cries of geese that ran loose on the property.

Parked in the carriage house was a 1958 Chevrolet pickup truck that had once been Mr. Ross's working vehicle on the farm. The doors had been removed and the tires had long since rotted out on the rusted rims of the wheels. Some late afternoons and evenings after dinner, I'd climb in and pretend to drive, imagining the route I'd take past Martinsburg into the mountains and the counties to the west and north of us. The seat's nylon cover was torn away, revealing foam and seat springs, so that they scratched against my bare legs as I sat with my left leg barely reaching the gas pedal and clutch and when I pulled the gear shift down on the steering column it made a wet popping sound that cracked in the still air of the carriage house. Mr. Ross used to say to me the truck had traveled more than 200,000 miles in its day, had been able to drive through any kind of weather so that he swore it possessed near-mythical powers, and I believed he was telling me the truth. Sitting in its cab, the eastern pasture visible in the dip through the chestnut and maple trees that lined the stone wall surrounding the front of the house, I'd read from the tattered copy of the *New Testament* I'd stolen from the Ross family library downstairs off the main dining room. Sometimes I'd read from the same parts my mother had once read to me, *Corinthians* or *Romans*, more often from the Gospels, and I would read silently to myself, the words passing my lips in silent syllables, near soundless, so that movement of my body came near to its accidental center, as if I could watch myself inside the cab and hear the sun moving past us and get creation's draw all over again through the liberties of this ghost language that filled the cab. "Truly, truly, I tell you, if one is not born from above, he cannot see the Kingdom of God. Nicodemus said to him: How can a man be born when he is old? Surely he cannot enter his mother's womb a second time and be born? Jesus answered: Truly, truly, I tell you, if one is not born from water and spirit, he cannot enter the Kingdom of God. What is born from the flesh is flesh, and what is born from the spirit is spirit. Do not wonder because I told you: You must be born from above." Looking out from the cab of the truck, the day passing into blue dusk, I'd sit with the pages of the book open on my lap, and there'd be the barking of one of the stray dogs that had once wandered onto the property and stayed, followed by the bleating of one of the two goats kept on the farm, and as the mourning doves sang from the trees just beyond the carriage house walls I'd notice that a kitten from the new litter had wandered under the porch of the house and not far distant from where it went the porch lights would come on and the roses on the trellis near the eastern part of the house would turn black inside the outlines of fading light.

 If I remained longer outside, I'd often observe the low flying bats whooshing past in the tranquil light of early dusk and then the cascading rip of voices from inside the house and dinner being made and Mrs. Ross standing on the porch like my own mother in a blue grey dress and cheap pearl necklace and her demeanor would be that of some vigilant matron and she'd stand the minutes it took to see through the failing light that I was still sitting in the cab of the vehicle and would call out to me then to come in. And sometimes I would and sometimes I wouldn't, preferring the solitude of the abandoned truck to what was awaiting me inside, and would continue reading from the text that lay in my lap like a soft bundle of wet fabric. "This is the judgment, because the light came into the world and people loved the darkness more than the light because their actions were wicked. For everyone who does bad things hates the light, lest his actions be discovered; but he who accomplishes the truth comes toward the light, so that it may be made clear that his actions were with God." When I closed the book and made my way up to the house, I could feel a low breeze against my legs and arms, like cool water spreading over my body, and Mrs. Ross had already turned to go back inside and behind me the pasture fell away from view into the late shadows of evening.

One night after dinner I wandered down to the library on the first floor at the front of the house, something that was forbidden all of us, except for the Ross's two sons. As I entered the room, the light was coming in from the gallery windows that fronted the portico and there was this smell of old leather and tobacco and wood smoke. On the shelves of the ceiling to floor bookcases were a set of Chambers's encyclopedia with the date 1874 stamped on each volume's leather spine, naturalist histories of the Shenandoah Valley, several books on local flora and gently worn, leather-bound editions of Dickens, Thackeray, James Fenimore Cooper and other writers I'd never heard of. Situated between the gallery windows was Mr. Ross's desk, a large oak affair that looked like something a wealthy lawyer might own. I sat down in Mr. Ross's leather chair from which he'd greeted all the new boys one morning, indicating that we were here for hard work and the kind of book learning that we hadn't yet had but would grow to appreciate. I slid open each drawer and viewed their contents of chewing tobacco containers and old coins and stamps and fingered a few of the coins, some of which had dates on them from just after the Civil War. In the bottom drawer, I found a wood-handled hunting knife with the initials J.L.R. carved into the handle. I opened the knife so that the silver blade shone in the light coming in through the windows, then closed the blade and shoved the knife into my pants and went back upstairs to the room where we all slept and stuck the knife in the bottom drawer of my dresser.

The next day Mrs. Ross came around as we sat in the playroom adjoining the kitchen and asked if any of us had something to tell her. No one said anything, until finally Jordan asked her why she was asking. Mrs. Ross turned her gaze over in my direction, then back to Jordan and the others, and said, "Something's missing from John's library desk, and he wants to know who's responsible." The five o'clock chimes of the clock in the hall went off as we looked around at each other and Mrs. Ross took a notepad out from her pocket book and said, "Here, if one of you knows something you can write it down and leave it on the table."

A few days later Matt was in our room going through

everyone's things and brought out the knife from the bottom of my drawer.

"Where'd you get this?" he said.

"I don't know. I've never seen it before," I said.

"You're a liar," he said. "A liar and a thief."

"No, I'm not. I don't know how it got there."

"I expect my mom will have some answers for you when she sees this," Matt said and went downstairs to find Mrs. Ross.

She never did come up and later that evening before dinner I went outside and it was like darkness but not, and I rummaged in my bag for a piece of licorice and went down to the stone wall separating the western and eastern pastures, and looked over to the barn where I'd once found the sloughed-off skin of a rattlesnake. I listened for the other boys and Joe, but no one was around. I walked slowly back up to the house and looked through the window and saw everyone assembled around the table for dinner, and Jordan caught a glimpse of me through the window and smiled back and then put a forkful of food into his mouth. When I came in, Evan and a couple of the other boys snickered and made the gesture of a knife passing across a throat and then it all got silent again when Mrs. Ross came in from the kitchen and Joe behind her said, "The boy need a plate?" She motioned for him to take the plate into the other room where she had me sit down as Joe brought a plate of food in for me, lima beans and minute steak and a side of applesauce, and heard the sharp quiet of the boys in the other room while I sat and ate by myself. Occasionally I'd notice Joe watching me out of the corner of his eye from the kitchen, as I finished my meal.

After dinner as we were getting ready for bed, Mrs. Ross

came up with a set of sheets, pillow and blanket and said, "You'll be sleeping upstairs on the third floor for awhile," and I looked at her and said, "For how long?" and she said, "For as long as I say, until you accept responsibility for what you did."

I took the linens in my arms, walked out of the room, and saw Jordan as I passed him in the hall. He gave me a look that said he was sorry but he couldn't do anything for me. When I got to the third floor, I threw the sheets and pillow and blanket on the floor, flopped on top of them, and listened to the TV going in the Ross's bedroom downstairs. The third floor rooms were mostly empty now except for a few old steel spring mattress beds set against the walls and some metal bureaus that were pushed against the corners of each room. The low ceiling of the middle bedroom came down in odd fashion so that you couldn't fully stand up in some parts of it but had to bow down, careful not to bump your head. When you looked out of the windows, what you saw was the lay of the land as my mother used to say, you could see all the way across the farm's pond to the barn and the fields beyond and out past them I knew that there was a train that came early in the mornings, because Mr. Ross caught it from Martinsburg to work in Washington each day and came back on it each night.

One of the dogs was barking in the yard, and I saw the stars through the window pane that had been hand-blown at the end of the 19th century so that everything appeared as if curving away from you, as though you were looking through a prism and the light was reflected back to you from objects that no longer held their place in the world.

After I was sent to the third floor, the other boys understood what it meant and treated me accordingly. One afternoon I went down to the icehouses and Matt and his brother, Evan, followed me along with two of the other boys, Charley and William, lanky kids who'd come to the farm from the D.C. suburbs of Hagerstown and Alexandria respectively, and who generally kept a low profile through the days we were together. When they caught up with me, Matt said, "You'd like it if we left you alone, wouldn't you?"

"Yes, I would," I said.

Matt took one of my arms and Evan the other, while Charley and William stood nearby, neither one wanting to get involved but not moving away either, as Matt and Evan pushed me down onto the ground.

"Do you admit you took the knife?" Matt asked.

"I never took anything."

Evan spat at me, and his spit felt hot on my cheek.

Matt twisted my right arm behind my back and said, "You sure? You really sure?"

I shook my head and felt tears coming down my face, and Matt pushed his knee into my back and said, "You can steal other people's stuff and cry about it? You've been takin' stuff from everybody: me, Evan, even Jordan."

I could see Jordan, standing just a bit farther out from the group and his arms were at his side and his eyes were nearly shut, it looked like, from the sun or just because he couldn't look.

And it was as if I were already dead, already underneath the ground, as one then another would come to dig me out. Only it wasn't a digging out but more like a burial, so that I felt like all their hands together were laying my body down in earth that was covered in chicken shit and goat dung, and Matt pushed my face into it again and again, until I stopped moving and his brother said, "Let's go, he's got nothin'." Jordan stood there without saying anything but started to move away from the other boys, like he knew there was nothing he could do but was doing it by standing there. I caught his gaze, then turned my eyes back to face the inside of the ice house where I'd been told by Evan that years ago a kid had hung himself from one of the beams. Though who the boy was and when this happened or if the story was anything more than apocryphal I couldn't have said.

When I came back to the house I passed Joe on the way up the stairs to the third floor, and he looked at me and said, "Son, what you gotten yourself into?" and I said, "Nothing, I just fell." He watched as I went up the stairs and said, "Dinner's in an hour. You best clean yourself up."

When I went into the bathroom, I saw that my shirt had been torn, the new one my mother had sent from a new department store in Washington and chicken feathers had stuck to my skin and my face was smeared with dung.

SIXTEEN

My old life seemed distant, Iris and Richard far from any world I could connect to. I kept to myself as much as I could, tried to avoid getting into trouble with the other boys. I went out in the mornings and did my chores on the farm, collecting eggs from the hen house, feeding the sole pig owned by the Ross's, steering clear of the pair of St. Bernard dogs kept on the property, one of whom had lunged at me one afternoon when I looked at him too long and had bitten a small chunk of my cheek with his teeth.

Letters came from my mother each week, brought to my Mrs. Ross who traveled to the post office in Shepherdstown each morning to pick up the mail. When I got the letters they'd already been opened, though I never asked Mrs. Ross if she'd read them or not. I just assumed that she had and once, when I returned home for vacation and my mother asked me about money she'd sent me to buy stamps for my stamp collection I told her I never got any money. My mother's letters came at the end of weeks, Thursdays and Fridays mostly and some weeks there was no letter and I'd ask Mrs. Ross to go and check again and she'd come to me later in the day and look over at me and squeeze my shoulder with her hand and say, "Probably tomorrow" before going back to whatever she'd been doing.

Iris's letters were usually addressed "My darling Andrew" or "My darling little Andrew" and seemed intended as cheerful, informative write-ups of her and my father's lives together. But so often they were also filled with a sadness that I couldn't quite get at, could never quite identify yet knew was there, as if she were typing on her Royal words that had a double meaning, coded so that I had to ferret out understandings that were never explicit. Her words and phrases looped around in my head until I saw them like spirals of language building to a small plateau and there I could stand and see her more clearly, see the words that emerged from the blue and white paper that felt heavy in my hands each week as I lifted them up to the light and there was the honking of geese that had been moving in a wild rush across the sky when I lifted the pages and if her hand were near to mine I could have brought the smallness of each typed letter back to its rightful owner, finger by finger, as if there was a sort of alchemy to language, that it could empower even the slightest emotion or description, give us back a way toward some other world that existed parallel to the lived one.

In all the ways I could say to myself there was no way to believe that I had been brought here, left here, that neither my mother nor father seemed to want me enough to keep me. *We want only the best for you, Iris wants the best for you,* my father would say in those days leading up to my being brought to the farm. *But if that's true,* I wanted to say, *why can't I belong to you, why can't I live where I belong with my own family?* I'd never said anything, though, and my father's words soon merged with so many others I heard from this time in my life with Richard and Iris that I began to see that the world wasn't shaped by real language, but by these pieces of made-up and distorted language. The sentences sounded like they meant something but they really didn't. If I turned away for a moment, I knew another set of words would come and another after that and nothing would change.

As the days of that fall and the next spring came and went, I began to believe that my mother and father would never come and get me, that my mother's letters were in their way designed to hide the actual reality here: *I had been abandoned again by those who had asked for me said they wanted me.* And how could that be so? Why had they brought me to them in the first place only to abandon me to this other family whose name was like mine but not, whose home was not my home, whose very being I could never translate into the vocabulary of home.

Reading my mother's words, I so often felt that it was as if language were in disguise. "I am hoping to see you soon," grew into sentences that went on for pages, partly real, partly invented, as if in catching one part of a sentence another emerged and another after that, each part growing larger than the last until the pages were covered in a kind of red writing, the typing erratic, emphatic, rushing across the pages like blind script from a letter my mother could not have written but that I would have to invent by my own hand, writing it into existence when it had never existed before.

When my mother's letters came, in those first minutes after Mrs. Ross delivered each one into my hands it was as if I was pausing time, taking a time-out from time, moving with my own mother again, the rhythms of her life, not mine, taking over. The light would shift in whatever room I was sitting in and the voices would be subordinate to the sound of the geese outside moving across the front yard and lower still would be the sounds of hens inside the henhouse and still lower would be the barely discernible distant shouts of the Ross boys chasing one of the other kids across the lower pasture. And all this while I sat in the room remote from everything it was as if we became one through the words Iris had written, and what I said in return became the dark mirror to her seemingly bright reflections.

After reading each letter, I would return it to its envelope and sometimes Mrs. Ross would pass me by on her way to the Plymouth to head into Martinsburg for groceries and seeing me sitting alone in the cab of her husband's old truck she would half-smile at me, her black pocketbook jostling on her hip as she walked toward the car across the oyster shell driveway.

> 2906 Ordway Street, N.W.
> Washington, D.C.
>
> March 15 1967
>
> Darling Andrew:
>
> Only a few days away, now, and it will be Easter, and you will be coming home for the holidays!
>
> It will be so lovely seeing my Andy again and I certainly hope you haven't grown too tall meanwhile for you really are shooting up so fast. Are you eating as much as ever?
>
> How are all the animals? Are there any new additions?
>
> I don't think you need to bring too many clothes with you, but I daresay Mrs. Ross will decide what you should pack, and she will, of course, notify us the date and train schedule so that we can meet you at the Washington Station.
>
> There is a good circus currently performing here in the city - as I see from the TV advertisement though I am not sure whether it will still be functioning by the time you arrive. Anyway, there will be lots for you to do so you will have a lovely time.
>
> The kittie-cats are fine and as pugnacious as ever chasing each other around the house. I really feel sorry for Pearly because Blacky won't leave him in peace!
>
> Have you been having fine Spring weather? Yesterday evening we had a storm with thunder peals so loud they almost split your ear-drums!
>
> Darling, learn all you can and try and concentrate for that is most important and realize that learning is actually lots of fun, but essentially, be good.
>
> With my fondest love and kisses for my little one,
>
> Your own Mummy

2906 Ordway Street, N.W.
Washington, D.C.

April 1 1967

My darling little Andrew:

It was so wonderful having you at Easter time, going shopping together like old times and having fun, making the log fire, and just sitting contentedly watching the different colors. Daddy gave me $10.00 towards the new clothes we bought for you, but I don't think he realized they cost much more. But never mind. You know, darling, the money I gave to you was for your piggy bank, and I never expected you to buy me a present. From the look of the package I think it is perfume but I don't want to open it because it might destroy your wonderful note to me: "Deary Mommy; I love you dearly. Love, Andy". To me, this is the most precious present I could ever wish to receive. Let me kiss you for it, sweetheart, and when you come home in June for summer holidays, I will open the package and then I will really know whether it is scent!

Daddy says there might not be a family visiting day before the summer vacations. If this is so, we will both have to wait patiently until we all are together.

Meanwhile, be my own good boy, pay attention and learn as much as you can — and no mischief, mind?

With all your Mummy's love, hugs and kisses

God bless
Mommy

2906 Ordway St. N.W.
Washington 8 D.C.

April 12 1967

My darling Andrew:

On April 20th you will be 9 years old! I am saying to you "Happy Birthday my sweet one". How I wish I could be with you to share a piece of your birthday cake, but when you blow out the candles say a wish and a prayer that we will all be together very soon - in June, as a matter of fact when you come home for the summer holidays.

For a present, I am not giving you more toys and more books; instead, I am sending herewith $2.00 for your stamp collection. Of course, you may spend it how you wish though I would prefer you not to buy chocolates and you have enough model cars at home. You are growing up now and stamp collecting is not only educative - it is a fascinating hobby.

Now the weather has changed in Washington for the better, the first Spring daffodils are blooming in the garden and just because you always liked to pick flowers for me, even in the surrounding gardens where you had no right to be, I did gather them together with some violets blossoming among the lawn.

I miss you very much, my Son, as I know you miss me. Be good, learn as much as you can and always remember that consideration, kindness and gentleness are the greatest assets and attributes for now and for all your future.

With my adoration, my kisses and hugs and all my love;

Your own,
Mummy

There is no hint in my mother's letters of the circumstances that had led to my being sent to what my mother would often refer to as "the Ross place." No sense of my having been banished or that, in ways my mother's letters hint at but don't say directly, relations between my mother and father had reached an impasse. Her wording suggests that they were together living at Ordway Street, in some fashion still together as husband and wife. I don't have any letters from my father from this period, so I have no way of knowing more than what my mother's letters relate. Spring is coming. We will soon be together. My mother is recovering from her fall on the ice. My father is being kind to her, giving her money for clothes for me. On April 20th I will turn 9 years-old. The woman who wrote these letters appears caring, warm, adoring even of her son. No evidence here of the mother who admits she cannot love him.

Like a landscape that seems filled with both light and shadow at the same time, my mother's letters provoked in me a sense of waywardness and longing. It was as if by looking long and hard at the light-filled areas of the field I might be able to walk only there, apart from the shaded areas that provided the landscape its more intricate meanings.

SEVENTEEN

While Matt and Evan and the other boys at Wild Goose left me alone after that day out by the ice houses, I knew what I wanted and needed most was a friend, someone to watch over and protect me. It seemed to me then that the days fell dark in bolts of black, shallow light, down to the door frames, and I'd be caught after dinner staring into the yard, as Joe would come out and say to me, "You not in bed yet? You get on inside before Mrs. Ross comes out," and I'd look off and his hand would gently nudge my body toward the stairs at the back of the house and I'd go up the back stairs to the third floor of the house, which is where the family that once owned the house in the 1930's had kept their children at night.

There were owls in the trees you could listen to and in the daylight breaking over the farm there was mist rising from the pond and the hollowed-out frame of the carriage houses where I went each evening after dinner. But there was no one there and when I looked down and heard the voices coming back up in the darkness, those of Mrs. Ross's or Matt or Evan or one of the other boys, it was like a journey was being taken without me and what I meant to know, what I needed to know, was where I fit, what I could do to be part of some family.

Even as I was kept apart from the other boys and rarely permitted to spend time with them beyond class and meal times, Jordan was becoming like an older brother to me. He had turned fifteen that summer, his face girl-like and pale as I remember it, his skin fairer than mine, his cheek bearing a small scar under his left eye from a childhood injury. His hands were delicate-boned, with a fineness that I associated with my mother's hands, so that as he spoke they would move through the air as if to emphasize a point he was making. Often, I'd notice the tapered paleness of his fingers that always seemed to be working with a piece of rope or string or whittling small bits of wood with his hunting knife, as he had started teaching me to make kites from balsa strips and colored tissue paper and string in one of the empty rooms on the third floor near where I slept. He called it the kite room, had been coming there since his first days at the farm, had made it a workroom for building his kites, though no one else referred to it that way. During one of my first nights on the third floor, I'd found Jordan at work on one of his kites and when I came into the room, he looked over at me and said, "How you holding up, kid?" and I said, "Best as I can," and he said, "Yeah, that's probably right," and turned back to his kite. I sat and watched him for awhile and asked him how long it took to make a kite.

"Depends," he said.

"On what?"

"Depends on the kind. Regular triangle kite you can finish in an afternoon. Box kites take longer, need more time to get all the parts to fit the way they need to."

I came over and watched him working for a bit longer before he turned and said, "You're not going to take anything, are you?" and I said, "Why would I do that?"

"Just be sure you don't," he said

I looked out the window, then back toward Jordan, and said, "I wouldn't do that," and he clipped a piece of nylon from a length of balsa.

"No, I don't think you would," he said.

Not long after, Jordan started spending more time in the kite room, and I'd come up to find him already at work. "Here," he'd begin, "you cut the strips of wood with this," handing me a small saw, "and like this you trim the strips as you need. Then you put the glue on each end and attach them, forming a T," and he would direct my hands with his, so that we were making the T of the cross bar together. "After you've done that," his left hand directing my hand into place over the cross-beam, "you apply some more glue onto the strips like this," tracing with his index finger a seam of white glue down the balsa strip, "and you fold the paper over the edges like this, making sure to cover the area between top and bottom of the T with the tissue, careful that you don't tear it while gluing it into place." His hands and mine would smell of glue afterward, and we'd wash together in the bathroom and return to the room to look over our work.

There wouldn't be words between us most days, not really, we didn't seem to need to say much to one another, and sometimes he'd come over to me and put his arm around me and once he bent his body into mine and kissed me on the lips so that I tasted licorice and tobacco after and I didn't move one way or the other, just watched his hand move through the light like a small diaphanous fan, ribbed and smooth at the same time.

I'd come up early one morning to fish with Jordan, left my room to walk down the pasture path out to where the creek bed was and the water stagnant and shallow, barely moving, and when Jordan saw me come through the trees he'd said, don't be stupid, there aren't any fish to catch here, put your rod down. It was just after daybreak and no one else had come down and he said, "You should be careful if they find out."

"I don't care, let 'em," I said, and he shook his head but didn't say anything.

I was still catching my breath from running down to the creek and he said, "Doesn't matter, the fish are gone."

"Then why'd you come."

"Because it's peaceful here."

"Yeah, that's true but why come out here when there aren't any fish?" He leaned over the creek bed like he was going to fall in and pulled his hand from his pocket and said, "It's easier, you know, if you don't think so much."

I didn't say anything but held onto my pole and let the lure float just above the surface and watched the nylon play out until the lure was downstream a ways. When I turned around Jordan had unrolled his bedding on the ground and was staring out over the creek.

I said, "What you doin'?"

"Lettin' the light do its thing," he said.

I took my rod and put it on the ground next to his and leaned over and he handed me a piece of bread and some cheese he'd brought with him and said, "It's all I've got but take some," and I said, "Thanks," and took the bread and a piece of cheese from his hand and saw the line of light come up across the horizon in one pink band, as I spotted a minnow moving inside the stream.

Jordan sat up and said, "Leave it go," and I watched it go silver and black over the stone surface as he took a knife out of his pocket and cut into the small block of cheese and passed me another piece.

"You see," he said, "there's this way we can connect to what isn't ours. It's all about seeing where you don't live yet, then coming to it and living there for awhile until you can say you're ready for anything that comes, you could die there and it would be ok. It's all about the way you let it let go from you and you go to it, so it's like you're underwater, and it's always going to be what you aren't that's most important, the part of you that isn't, that's what you listen for and move toward, that's how you know where you are in the world."

I was part of what wasn't, he said, and he trusted me for being that, for being that thing that wasn't expected or known and I knelt down and skimmed a rock off the water's surface so it broke across the surfaces in several places at once. I let the water slide off my wrist and when I took it out of the water it was slick from the creek and I let another rock go in one arc over the dead near-silent creek bed and when I looked up I saw the empty space where Jordan had been waiting for me.

One afternoon after we finished building two new kites, his a yellow and orange box kite, mine a traditional diamond kite of red and white paper, we went to the window together and looked below to see Evan and Matt Ross in the pasture, helping some of the other local boys from Shepherdstown bale hay, their white t-shirts moving above the hay bales like sails on a moving tide, and beyond them were the fields that led to the road we took to go into town. I was watching them disappear as I'd done countless afternoons before and remembering as I watched them how hard it had been at times to stay here, how many times I'd wanted to run away, not sure where I'd go, who would come find me, where I'd end up. And in that calmness, like someone who could see things going on and didn't need words, Jordan took my hands in his and patted then kissed one then the other, and I let him press them together. He said this was what good friends should do, they should show each other how they felt. It wasn't much, the touch of his hands on mine was warm and comfortable, like my mother's hands moving over mine in the cold so that she'd warm them with hers, saying "Cold dannies" as she did so.

"How do you feel?" he said, and I looked over at our kites then into his green eyes, one of his lids lower than the other like my own low left lid, and I said, "You're my friend."

"That's right, I am," he said and he took me into his arms in a bear hug, then turned me slowly like I was being enfolded and encircled at the same time, and we seemed almost to fall together onto the floor, his body falling on top of mine. I saw a crease of light beneath the door that was shut now, then the folds of light from the window that was partly open so that a cool breeze came over me as Jordan laid me on the mattress. His hand slid under my belly and he undid my shorts and pulled them down around my ankles, and I could hear him behind me unzipping his pants and pulling them down too, and then he spread my legs apart and asked, "Is it ok?" and I watched the dust motes floating above my head from the sunlight coming through, and I said, "Don't make me wet," because I remembered reading about how boys had fluid that flowed out of them when they got excited and I didn't want that feeling down there. He pushed himself into me and it hurt at first, then I let go and he was inside me, and there was the smell of cornflower all around me, and his hands held onto mine as he jerked forward and backward.

As he moved on top of me, I kept looking across the room where the light was now falling across the boards and saw a brass nail head that needed to be struck back into place. I felt something burn inside me and tried to pull out from under him, and Jordan held onto my torso for a moment, then shifted his body weight off me and when I turned over he was already putting his pants back on and had made his way to the other side of the mattress.

"Did I hurt you?" Jordan asked.

"No, it's okay," I said because I knew that he'd meant no harm, that what he'd done was something he viewed as a secret between us, a kind of bond we could share. He kissed me on the cheek when I sat up, and I turned away from him so that I was facing the window and saw that it was getting still and quiet outside as it always did on the farm this time of afternoon.

Outside it was sort of a half light that fell over the landscape, and I saw myself in it and the room was filled with shadow and the sun was low across the trees, everything was going back to its settled place, and later I would go outside when everyone else was asleep and look up into the morning sky and watch the meteors come flying across the horizon like flares that wouldn't stop. I remembered the story of Cain and Abel I'd read in Sunday school and how short a time it was that they lived before Cain slew Abel in the field and the light was hard that day on Cain's back as his face was averted from God and he knelt down low to the earth and saw his brother's blood flow into the wet ground and the stars came high over his head and the light was complete when he saw what he'd done and heard that his crime would not go unpunished, he would be an exile for the rest of his days, never to pass homeward again.

EIGHTEEN

Over the next several weeks, the kite room became a kind of sanctuary, an unreal space without borders or time or connection to the world below. Often, I went there by myself and waited for Jordan to come up and I'd sit with the kite-making materials and hear the doves in the eaves long past morning. I wasn't made yet; I wasn't an "I" yet. I felt more like something made of paper and string, like the kites Jordan and I made, I was exactly like the kites, able to fly above the house where I'd been left, above these rooms without walls, this space that occupied my senses but left my body incomplete. And once I recalled the words of Isaiah: "Wash yourselves and ye shall be clean; put away the wicked ways from your souls before Mine eyes; cease to do evil; learn to do well. Seek judgment, relieve the oppressed, consider the fatherless, and plead for the widow. Come then, and let us reason together, saith the Lord: Though your sins be as scarlet, I will make them white as snow; and though they be red like crimson, I will make them white as wool." And when I turned my body around, I knew that I was put here to wait. But for what?

One night followed the next in those days when I was still being kept apart from the other boys and left to spend nights by myself on the third floor, brought down for meals and lessons during the day, then sent back up. I heard the birds passing overhead, the sounds of a house that wasn't at rest but moving toward it as each day completed itself and a new one came to take its place. Resting on my bed through those long nights I listened for those who might come to get me, to take me back to wherever it was I belonged. From my bed, I stared off into the dark and the door that was left ajar and heard sometimes the passing overhead of a plane, then nothing. Downstairs was a world I didn't know and above me the heavens were marked by small points of light set back against a background of black fabric. And when I lay down again it could be nightfall or the morning after. The wind could be southerly or westerly, and above the doorjamb was the insignia of a family that no longer lived here. When I went out onto the landing and smelled the light filled with the heaviness of bacon fat, I would trace the wall seam with my eyes down to the first staircase, then the second, watching myself as one visits another from across the room, watching myself descend then disappear into the darkness of the rooms above.

Drifting off to sleep then no sleep, I laid awake and said to myself, it's coming to an end, this is all coming to an end, and it seemed perfectly strange, strangely perfect, the world underneath, like a watery space that was always there, always ready to receive you, and there was this opening, like the crawl space underneath a house, where you could go and taste the earth in your mouth again and smell the food being cooked above you and the light that found you was this restorative kind that seemed almost to lay down with you, to keep your body and head still when you heard movement up above.

Jordan disappeared for awhile, I don't know for how many days, but it seemed like a week, maybe more. It was late autumn by this point and the leaves were nearly gone from the trees and the white columns of the old plantation house had the appearance of rubbed marble in the light that came hard across the front most afternoons. Jordan had left or was taken away from the farm for reasons that I never learned. When he came back, it was late evening, and I saw him sitting by himself on the side of the house, in his lap a hunting rifle, and he was fingering the barrel when I came up and sat down next to him.

"Where'd you go?" I said.

"I've been around." Jordan looked over at me and smiled, but I wasn't sure.

"Around where?"

"Hereabouts."

"Yeah?"

"Yeah."

"You mad at me?"

Jordan shook his head and reached over to take my hand, and he said it was getting time for him to leave the Ross farm. He'd gotten word from his mom that her boyfriend had moved out and she couldn't afford the school anymore. I said that was a shame. He didn't look over but kept his gaze steady on the few geese left on the farm, and he ran his hand through his hair a couple of times.

"Yeah, but it's ok," he said, "I knew this would happen. Maybe it will be better with me at home this time."

"It's like a gift you've got back again," I said. "You must be glad you have a mom who's there and needs you."

"Yeah, sure, but you ..."

I cut him off and said, "Things aren't right, but they will be one day."

He just nodded.

Inside, it was near dinner time, and Jordan played with

the barrel of the gun while I looked over at the pond where a year before there'd been this light, like a spreading soft core of yellow across the surface, and now there was a dull silver hue to the water, as if water and pond weren't the same thing, as if one transformed inside the other but wasn't the other.

We got up to go, and I followed Jordan down the path behind the carriage house that led back out to the fields of the southern pasture. As we walked, I followed the power lines with my eyes and heard our footsteps in the wet grass moving in unison.

The last time I would see Jordan he came up to the third floor after dinner, and he sat on the bed opposite mine.

"I don't want you ever to forget that I'm your brother, no matter what," he said.

It came to me as he sat there that I didn't know what a brother was, had never had one, even as Jordan had adopted me in the kite room like I belonged to him.

"We're both orphans, I guess," I said, "like we don't have a proper place in the world."

He laughed and said, "It's not so much about being orphans, it's more like a road trip. You get to one place and set up your stuff and stay a little while and then it's time to move and do it all over again."

I thought what did it mean to have a brother in the world, even as I knew I had no brother, no one to say I was theirs and they were mine, only those who claimed we were all part of the same circle even as I knew that wasn't true.

Jordan looked over at me when I didn't respond.

"What you need to realize is that, whatever else, there'll

come a time when you and me will make sense," he said. "I never wanted it to be something you thought was wrong or bad."

"I know," I said. "I don't."

He glanced down at my hands.

"They've grown, they look more like a man's hands," he said.

I smiled and said, "I don't think so. They're still kid's hands as far as I can tell."

I didn't even think they showed callouses yet from the farm work we'd been doing through the fall, and part of me wished that they did.

Jordan pulled out a five-dollar bill.

"I bet you in a year you'll have a girlfriend," he said.

"I don't think so," I responded. "Have you ever had a girlfriend?"

"Not really, but I did some stuff with this girl once."

"Did you love her?"

He was silent, then said, "No, love wasn't part of it."

"I don't think I'll never find anyone," I said, "at least no one who stays."

He smiled and said, "It'll take time, for sure, but you've got plenty of that. You're all of, what, nine or ten, right?"

I laughed, and we sat there in the light and both laughed a little.

Jordan took my hands in his and stroked them and came to sit beside me on the bed and passed his right palm through my hair and said "Why don't we just lie down together?" He smelled like talcum powder and I said ok and he smiled and said he just wanted to lie down for a bit this last time and when he put his arm around me I turned to face the wall and saw the light go dense then pale across its surface and his hand reached over and pulled me into his body where I lay crumpled like a rag doll next to him.

When I woke in the middle of the night, Jordan was gone, and I walked through the rooms of the third floor looking for him and when I came into the kite room he was resting on the floor against the wall with the last box kite we'd made together held against his chest and I came over and took the kite from his arms and placed it on the work table and knelt down and adjusted his shirt collar that had been bent over and placed his arms one over the other like I'd seen them do with dead people in movies. I couldn't hear Jordan breathe but knew that his breath was there nonetheless, shallow and slow but there all the same, and left him to go back down the hall to the room where I slept.

I sat on the bed and stared out the window and waited for the sound of the B&O freight that passed through town each night, and when I woke next, it was daylight. I walked down the hall to the kite room. There was no sign of Jordan, only the kites we had made together.

NINETEEN

At holiday break, my father picked me up from Union Station and drove me back home in the cool winter darkness of D.C. When we got to our house, my mother was outside sweeping the front stoop, and when I came up the steps, she put the broom down long enough to come over and give me a hug and said, "Go inside, you'll catch your cold," and I carried my suitcase into the house that smelled of fireplace ash and soup on the stove. I went up to my room where the bed was made just as I'd left it in August.

When I came down, I saw the car was gone from out front, and my father had left. I asked my mother where he'd gone, and she said, "It doesn't matter, let me look at you." I stood in front of her in the living room, and she said I'd gotten taller, my features had changed, become more adult-like. I said I was the same, nothing had really changed. She lifted her glass and said, "We'll see." I followed her into the kitchen and out on the back porch where she said, "This is where I sit most nights waiting for you to come home, like the lost dog Sheba in that movie we watched together." I said, "I am home," and she said, "Yes, you are, yes you are." We sat there for a time on the porch looking out over the garden that was covered in a light frost, and she said, "What do you want to do tomorrow?" I said I didn't know, maybe see what was playing at the Uptown. We went back inside, and she put bowls of beef barley soup on the table for us, but didn't eat anything herself, just let her bowl get cold and sit in front of her while I ate.

"You'll need some warm clothes to wear back on the farm," she said, "I heard from Mrs. Ross you didn't bring anything warm for the cold weather."

"No," I said, "but I'm ok, I can wear the sweater you got me."

She said, "We'll see if we can't find something at Kaufman's," and pushed her plate away from her and got up from the table and went into the front room, where she sat down and pulled the bottle back from behind the curtain, forgetting I could see what she was doing, and said, "I'm more tired than I thought, they said I should get more rest, but your father—"

She lifted the bottle of Scotch to her lips and took a swig. "Your father is losing his patience with me, I don't think it's fair but that's what I get for marrying the man when I was still too young to know better," and she took another swig from the bottle and put it down, and said, "Come over here, darling, let me look at you," and set the bottle back behind the curtain before going on, "I'm just not resting enough is all. I've only so much energy left, not enough, no doubt, not enough, but you and I will have some time now to do things, won't we?" The question hung there between us, and I didn't respond but sat on the couch beside her as the light from outside shifted, becoming greyer.

She glanced around the room as if looking for someone else, and I said to her, "What is it?" and she said, "It's nothing, I thought you were going to—" then paused and said, "It's good you've come home."

My mother stood up from the couch slowly and carefully, and I put my hand out to steady her, but she waved me off and said, "No, my darling, I'm fine," and went into the hallway and up the stairs. I could hear her go up the landing and down the hallway into her room and close the door and throw her shoes off and lay herself on the bed. When I went up a little while later, I imagined she'd already fallen asleep, the light was out from underneath the door, and I couldn't hear anything from inside her room. I went down the hall into my room and took the last kite that I'd made with Jordan out of my suitcase and put it on the windowsill so that the fine white and red paper caught the light. I lay on the bed watching the kite for awhile until it became like a phantom bird I could follow through the night sky, and the higher it flew the harder I had to look to see it until finally it disappeared altogether.

When I woke, the kite rested unmoving on the sill, and I lowered the blind and let the darkness enfold everything around us.

TWENTY

When I returned from West Virginia at the end of the school year, the heavy days of summer had begun again. School was out and memories of my time at Wild Goose Farm, Mrs. Ross, Jordan and the other boys—all of it had already started to fade. I was inside again, inside the rooms I'd left that hadn't changed much in my absence: my mother's cats still roamed the house waiting for her to come down and feed them, the dining room where my mother had typed the letters I'd gotten at the farm, the hallway leading to my room with the splintered pieces that still caught on my feet as I made my way back to my bedroom.

My father had now officially moved out and taken a place of his own, two rooms in the Quebec House apartment complex that was about two and a half blocks from our house. "It's for the best," my mother had said to me one of those first mornings I was back in the house and there was no way to avoid his absence. I'd gone up to his room, opened the door, peered in...nothing on the desk but the light that had never functioned properly, some tax papers my mother had been looking through, a few pencils, unsharpened, lying near the sharpener.

"When will he come back?" I asked my mother, aware that even as I posed the question there wasn't likely to be any kind of real response that made much sense of this new stage of my parents' marriage.

"We don't know, perhaps in a few months," my mother said, putting another pot in the sink to soak in the dish soap.

I brought a plate in from the dining room and placed it on the counter next to the sink.

"It will be you and I for awhile, so I need you on your best behavior. Whatever happens, you need to help me here. God knows, no one else will."

"Yes, Miss Ross," I said out of habit, then corrected myself, "mums."

"Mrs. Ross?" my mother said sharply. "Really? You think I look like that sad poor woman from the farm?"

"No," I said. "I'm just used to speaking to her all the time."

My mother took the pot out of the sink, placed it on the counter to dry.

"And what? She's still in your head, still taking care of you? I don't think so."

"I'm sorry," I said.

"Christ, Andy."

"I know."

"Do you? Do you really know?"

"Well, I can't know everything, but I know that I should know my own mother from a stranger."

Iris's face had become still, as if whatever I said couldn't make any kind of difference.

"I'm tired," she said. "Let me go lie down for a bit. We'll see what to do about dinner later."

"Yes, mums," I said and watched my mother go upstairs. I went down the back steps and out the gate and into the alley. No one was around, the street still and heavy from the humidity. Down on Connecticut Avenue the D.C. Transit buses roared into gear and the mourning doves were making that sound that always reminded me of home. Up the hill a stray dog made its way toward Highland Place, while behind me I could feel the sun moving through the leaves of the 125-year-old oak that rose above our house.

I came back inside and let the screen door fall shut behind me and went to my room and waited for my mother to wake from her nap.

June 7 was a Friday. The heat had come up with the morning light and hadn't stopped. By 3 p.m. our thermometer hanging from the den window showed the temperature as close to 100. I was supposed to spend the weekend with my mother, according to the arrangement that she and my father had agreed to, but that seemed to have as many exceptions as regularities and I quickly gave up trying to make plans one way or the other.

"Yes, Andy," my father had said to me, "you must stay with mummy and be good to her. Be a good boy. Show her you will cooperate. Yes?" I only understood that he and my mother had made this arrangement, as they had done with Wild Goose Farm, and it was one that I had little say in.

Around three that afternoon my mother sat down and poured her first glass of Scotch, then said, "Why don't you make some lemonade for us?"

"Yeah, okay," I said, to which she said, "Yes, it's 'yes' not 'yeah'." I nodded and went into the kitchen and poured the powder into the pitcher we'd had for as long as I could remember and threw some ice cubes in and filled it and brought the pitcher and glasses back to the living room.

She'd finished her drink when I came back into the room, and the door was open to the street. She sat to my right while I rested on the floor and drank the lemonade with her and watched her get tired from her drink. She'd already poured another from a bottle behind the drapes and thought no doubt that I didn't see her pull the bottle out since I'd been out of the room. It was by this point a familiar game we played: she pretended that nothing had happened, and I pretended that I hadn't seen what she'd just done.

Her face got that still look it had after her second or third drink, and I saw it wouldn't be long. I asked if she wanted to lie down, and she looked up at me, as if surprised to find me still standing there in the room with her.

"It's remarkable really how quickly things can change, wouldn't you agree?"

"I don't know," I said, wary of whatever was coming next.

"Just remarkable. I thought—we both thought—well—having a child is never easy. No, never easy."

I played with a book of matches left on the table, as my mother reached out to grab them out of my hand. "You never made it easy for us, did you? Always the hard way. You're the reason he's not here, you know. He'd rather not be here, and I don't blame him. I wouldn't be here either if I didn't have to be, I can = tell you that, buster."

"Where would you be, mums?" I asked, careful to keep my distance. The light was changing behind us, now a slow orange band forming on the carpet between the sofa and the wall behind her.

"Oh god. Not here, Christ, not here. In this fucking lousy country that treats its people like garbage. This basin of filth called America. No, thank you. I'm going back to England. Already have my passport ready to go. Your father can take care of you. I'm done trying."

If I had believed in God, I would have prayed for that day to come as soon as possible.

"And what did I think anyway?" Iris went on and I knew it would be another sermon on lost chances, lost possibilities, and there'd be nothing I could say or do but stand there the time it took for her to repeat these stories I'd heard a hundred times over. "Marrying a Pole with hardly any English, coming to this country to make things better for him, settling in this godforsaken backwater of a city. Then you—" Iris looked me in the eye for the first time since she'd been talking. "Yeah, *you*. Which wasn't my choice, I can tell you. Was trying for a British baby. Told him that's what we should get. A sweet English girl. Something to be thankful for. Instead, well… He told me there wasn't a way for us to adopt. The English weren't letting their orphans go overseas. I told him, 'Rubbish.' But he said it was the only way. So, we go looking at pictures, tons of pictures of little brown babies from India, West Africa, even some kids from this country. We ended up picking Greece, the only place then in the business of sending their babies out of the country. Best we could do. And he picks you out like a puppy from its litter. Says to me, 'this one.' I said, 'he doesn't even look Greek.' 'This one,' he says, 'I want this one for my son.' I said to him, 'You want him, you can go get him. But don't expect me to treat him like my own.' Who knew, right? That I would turn out to be right. Well.…"

She turned and lifted the bottle of Scotch from behind the drapes and opened its cap and took a swig, then replaced the bottle behind the drapes. The light came in for a moment, flashed then darkened. "So, here we are, Andy, just you and me. And your father, well, he's got better things to do, I guess, than be here—"

"You want to lie down?" I interrupted her.

"Doing what he should as a father, which isn't his way. No, not his way. Better just to leave, leave me and you to fend for ourselves. Isn't that right, darling?"

"I don't know," I said. "I think daddy wants us to have a good time."

My mother laughed and said, "Oh, and we are, aren't we, yes we are." She looked into the glass of lemonade and glanced back up at me. "You shouldn't have—" the words slurred slightly as they came out, "taken it away."

"Taken what, mums?" I asked.

"It's good. I'm going to sleep. You can take me to bed now."

I held my hand out to her, and she reached for it, before letting it go. "Stupid," she said. I stood beside her as she raised herself from the sofa, and helped her into the hallway and up the stairs to her bedroom. The light was soft, like the light that formed just above the surface of a swimming pool, and we were like two people underwater together.

"Turn it on for me," she said, pointing to the air conditioner.

"Okay, mums," I said, and helped her onto the bed, then lifted her legs until they were on top of the sheet.

"You want to be covered?"

She didn't answer, her eyes already closed and her breathing heavy. I left the room and went back downstairs, where I took the glasses from the table and brought them with the pitcher into the kitchen, lay everything carefully in the sink, and walked around for awhile, not sure whether I should leave my mother sleeping or wait until she woke.

I listened for any sound of her, but none came. An hour or so I wandered around the downstairs, moving between the kitchen and the den and back to the living room again. For the first time since she'd gone to sleep, I thought of what my mother had said to me. I knew none of it would matter the next day, that she wouldn't even remember half of it, if any part at all. It was like the world was made of these broken pieces that slid into view every so often, then slid back, becoming invisible again. But you knew they were always there, wouldn't ever be gone. You just had to wait for them to come out again. It didn't matter, I said to myself, none of it matters. Not a word of it would change anything.

A little after 7 by the mantle clock, I went out onto the front porch, looked over at the row houses across the street, the trees heavy and low over the wires that crossed in front of their windows. Mr. Lopez was sitting on his stoop and looking over at a group of young women who were now passing up the street, on their way back from shopping, their arms full of groceries in Safeway bags, and between them, a young boy of about ten was pushing his skateboard. Further down the street, near the corner of 29th, our neighbors had turned on their outdoor light, the glow barely visible, mixed, muted with the early evening light that had the feel of talcum to it, powdery, dust-like, still on the hands and arms and faces of those passing up the street.

I left the porch and walked down the hill toward the avenue. The clock over Riggs Bank said it was 7:07. It was still Friday, and I wondered when my mother would wake and what she would see when she did, the house dark so that it would fill up with shadows, wondered if she would notice at first that I'd gone, that I wasn't there, how long that would take her.

When I got to my father's apartment, he wasn't there. I wandered into his bedroom and saw that his bed was still unmade and on the floor beside it were his Polish newspapers that I guessed he'd been reading the night before. I went back into the living room and came over to the bay window facing east toward Porter Street and stared off into the evening light as if there was little else in the world to see or do, no other place I could know that would make a difference to anyone.

TWENTY-ONE

Much of what happened inside the house that night and the next day, between the time I left my mother on Friday and that Sunday afternoon my father and I came back, seemed, as I thought of it later, inevitable, a sort of prelude to what would come to pass only four years later. I'm told that often, in the days leading up to a suicide attempt, people will act in the same way they always do, will go through the same patterns during the day, but at a certain point, it's like a switch gets thrown and the moment presents itself as an out. It's said there are ten minutes that make all the difference between following through and not. The person sees the chance to go—and either takes it or lets the opportunity pass. I've often thought that for Iris at different points along the way in her lifetime, there must have been several such passages of time, minutes in which she considered her options: to stay or go. And most of the time, she'd opted to stay. But the choice was never gone for long, and when it came back, like a wind that wouldn't stop forcing tree branches up against the side of the house, how long before the wind unsettled those branches, breaking off first one then another?

On Saturday my father and I went to Safeway on the corner of Ordway and Connecticut Avenue and bought groceries for my mother, things she'd apparently told my father she needed when he last spoke to her on the phone the day before. We came up to the house and knocked on the door, but my mother never answered. We left the bags propped up between the inner and screen doors and went back to my father's apartment for lunch. Later that day, my father tried several times to call, but she never picked up. We went to bed that night not sure what to do, what had happened.

The next morning we rose early, and my father came into the living room where I was sleeping on the couch.

"We should go and see what has happened," he said. "Maybe something has happened to Iris."

My father seemed both worried and resigned to whatever we would find once we came to the house. We left the apartment and walked across Porter Street and up the back alleys to our house. The bags of groceries we'd delivered were still sitting there between the screen and front doors, and we stood for a time on the second set of steps before moving onto the porch, as if at any moment my mother would come out. But she didn't. We knocked and heard nothing from inside, dead still. Behind us nothing was moving either, the heat heavy and damp, as it had been from the day before, somewhere close to 85 degrees at 10 in the morning. I looked over my shoulder at my father who was peering into the top windows of the door now and pushing at it, since he didn't have a key anymore. His weight fell hard against the door that seemed to be double-bolted from inside.

We went around back and heard the neighbors in the house next door arguing as they had been doing regularly lately and passed the side door to the basement and kept moving past until we came to the little gate that led into the back garden. I searched for the key under the ledge, but it wasn't there. Did he know yet what we would find? He went up the stairs of the back porch and knocked on the panes of the back door, and again, there was no sound from inside. He came back down and joined me in the garden, saying, "If she is gone, she would have told us," and it was then that she appeared from behind a curtain, just her face there for an instant, peering out at us.

"Look," my father said, "Iris is here." The door opened, and my mother appeared on the top step, barely recognizable in her torn nightgown, her legs and feet streaked with blood.

"Iris, what did you do?" She nearly fell into his arms, and my father turned toward me.

"Quickly, Andrew, go inside and call an ambulance."

When I went in, the air smelled heavy, acrid, from the combined odors of sweat, fried fish, and urine. I saw a stash of bottles pulled from behind the drapes and lining the wall in the dining room. Unwashed dishes had been left in every room it seemed, and at first, I couldn't find the phone, as it had been thrown behind some books on the floor.

The ambulance arrived shortly after and the paramedics placed Iris on the steel gurney and carried her down the stairs and lifted her into the vehicle. "You should come," my father said.

"No, it's better if I stay here. I'll just wait until you get back."

It was a little after 12 noon as I watched the ambulance go up the hill on Ordway, its siren and lights going, and my father was in the back with her. I was in the house watching from the porch when they disappeared in the heat and light of afternoon, the clouds passing like straw panels above, so that every brick across the way seemed sharp, marked by the fiery light.

The landing window that overlooked our neighbor's house

had been shattered, and glass fragments lay on the landing covered in blood—the result I assumed of my mother falling down the stairs. Some of the bannister rungs had come loose and seemed to hang like torn tendons in the light streaming in through the broken window. In my mother's room, her bed had scorch marks from where a fire had started, the sheets and mattress burned through in parts. A pitcher that smelled as if it had been used as a urinal rested near the bed on its side, and the copy of Shakespeare's *Collected Plays* that my mother often read lay beside the bed along with a bra, underwear, some discarded stockings worn at the heels and toes. On the dresser near the window, the drawer where my mother kept her pills—sleeping aids, pain medication—was open, and the pill boxes all emptied out, caps loose on the bottom of the drawer next to the slender plastic containers.

This must have been what she wanted, I thought, as I looked around the room, *not to wake up, this must have been the point, not to come back, to let fire consume her, let sleep take her.* Would it have mattered had I stayed, not gone back to my father's, not left her? Would she have sat up and recognized me standing in the hallway in the middle of the night, looking in, waiting, not certain what would happen next, but knowing I needed to keep watch?

Who can say? I sat down on the floor and let the light fall across my body and waited for my father to come get me.

TWENTY-TWO

In the weeks after what my father referred to as "Iris's accident," my mother took to bed for days at a time. I was left to care for her, just as I was made to understand that my mother's fall and the aftermath could have been prevented had I stayed with Iris. "You should never have left," my father said to me, "you know how she could become..." his voice trailing off, as if to say that the worst was always possible and I should have known that, should have been alert to the signs, remained with her until she woke up.

The bandages on my mother's legs and left foot needed changing several times a day, a task that became mine, since we couldn't afford a nurse and my father had returned to Quebec House and came by every other day or so to check on us. He would bring groceries sometimes, often a bottle of wine he would open and drink with Iris in the living room before returning back to his apartment. My father would smile wanly as my mother told him again and again of her desire to return to England, her face brightening as she recalled the London of her youth, and he would say, "Yes, Iris, of course, one day we will do this," until her hand would smack hard on the glass table and she'd look at him as if he'd only just appeared, and he would say nothing at all, nothing to comfort or confront her, just wait for the mood to pass.

What had happened that June day? As early summer became late summer and fall, my mother talked of my having tried to kill her. "You tried to murder me," she said. "Tried to poison me with sleeping pills."

"No, mums," I said, "you took them yourself. I wasn't here and you took them, then set the bed on fire from your cigarette."

"Help me with this," she said, stripping off a layer of gauze that had become bloody and yellow. "I know you did it. You can admit it. It's okay. You can tell me."

"I didn't do anything," I said. "I came back with daddy, we found you like that."

Her hand pushed mine away as she rewrapped her foot. The fleshy part of her heel had been sliced away, it seemed, and was still raw, oozing yellow pus into the gauze. My father and I determined that the injury to Iris's foot came from her having fallen down the stairs and gone through the window on the landing. We'd found smashed glass pieces coated with her blood all down the stairs, with some pieces having been tracked into other parts of the house.

"Come, help me up," she said. "Come help me get down the stairs." Together, we walked back down the stairs and landing she'd fallen on, past the window that had been taped up with cardboard. "We need to get that fixed. I'll have to call Mr. Johnson to come repair it."

When my mother sat back on the sofa, she looked at me. Her voice softened for a moment. "You can't help yourself, I know. I know. You wanted your mums to die, yes. It's okay. It's understandable, the way you—"

She stopped, readjusted the bandage on her foot. "The way you have taken his side, stopped being my son. It's understandable. So, you tried to kill me. And I'm still here. You couldn't quite pull it off, could you?"

I looked down at the carpet and noticed for the first time the figure of a young woman crossing a bridge, the pattern of the weave creating a dark band of gold just over the woman's right arm. In one part of the weave, a clotted blue moon appeared while above the bridge silver birches appeared to droop near the ground.

"Go away," she said. "Can't stand the sight of you. Just go away, I don't care where. Just go."

"Yes, mums," I said and went out onto the porch and down the stairs and onto the street toward my father's apartment.

*

The story of what happened in the house to Iris during that weekend would shift repeatedly in my recollection over the years. It could never be perfected, was always traveling the same broken route, somewhere between memory and invention, between what I wanted to recall and what stood in the way of any memory at all... It was an afternoon in June, the magnolia tree in the alley had bloomed and its leaves had fallen, creating a deep layer of pink on the alley surface. My father is wearing a plaid shirt, frayed along the cuffs and collar. His face remains unshaven, and his hair lacking the usual weight of pomade he applied each morning. I am a little over a month past my ninth birthday. My hair had become matted with sweat, dark and falling onto my forehead in heavy bangs. I don't smile or make any visible gestures, as my father and I walk together up the stairs of the house.

Together, we walk around the front of the house through the narrow walkway bordered by a high fence. The back yard hasn't been cleared in weeks. The rose bushes have been torn out from their trellis by a rainstorm, and the petals are scattered around the bushes in a semi-circular fan. The lawn, usually mowed every few weeks by a neighborhood handyman, is rough and yellow and high and patches of earth now appear in some patches where the boy used to play soccer.

My father is walking through the yard up the stairs. He knocks on the glass pane and stands back. He listens at the door and motions to me. Hearing no sound from within, we move together down the small path that goes between the houses and leads to the front. My father goes first up the concrete stairs and stands on the porch. With one hand holding his newspapers and the other inside his pocket he looks into each of the windows. I have moved to a position near the gate leading to the alley and am looking over at the neighbor's house. Ivy has nearly covered one side of the brick face, and inside the house, I can see my mother pass the side window three times, each time pressing her face into the glass for just long enough for me to catch a glimpse of her. I don't know if she has seen me or if she understands why we have come. She seems confused, half-awake, passing back and forth in front of the window, and I motion to her while my father behind me listens for any sound from within.

My father has placed the paper on the floor of the porch and opened the screen door and knocked on the glass pane of the inner door. I have gone back down the stairs and stand at the edge of the yard and look up into the windows where I see my mother's hand move the drapes back into place. The drape is drawn slowly, not hastily. She is visible only for an instant, but the hand's movement makes a line across the edges of the frame. I advance across the lawn from the gate and walk down the three stairs to the sidewalk leading to the house, on one side of me the tall wood fence dividing our property from our neighbors'.

My father has cut his finger, and it has started to bleed. I offer him a handkerchief from my back pocket, but my father has put his finger in his mouth and pushes my hand away. He continues to peer into the house. He has left his newspaper on the bottom step and taken from his pocket a set of keys. The keys make a jangling sound, like wind chimes in a slow breeze. I move toward the steps and hear the door inside the house being opened, then closed again.

My father has taken the keys out of the lock and is opening the door, then closing it. He sees in the kitchen that nothing has been touched, the plates have been left on the drain board, the fruit bowl is filled with the remnants of Jello from the week before. I settle on the bottom step of the porch and wait while my father moves into the darkness. On the ground next to my right leg I find an empty glass and place it upright in the grass. A red ant emerges at the inner rim of the glass and begins to make its way up the side. When it reaches the top it drops back down into the grass and begins to climb back up again.

The basement window is level with my eyes, and I can see that there is a light on inside. Someone has left a light on in the basement, or it has just been switched on. When I look up I see my father has now entered the dining room of the house. My mother stands near the door to the bathroom, and my father and she are now standing together. I am on the porch looking through the window.

I stare down at the glass and the ant making its way

back down the side. My father has returned to the kitchen, followed by my mother who is mumbling something I can't catch. Nothing has been touched. The plates have been left on the drain board, the fruit bowl filled with the remnants of Jello. Standing on the top step, I watch the two figures moving through the shadows of the kitchen. My mother has a kitchen towel wrapped around her right foot and gauze that has become heavy and thick with blood wrapped around the shin of her left leg. My father is standing near her and has the telephone in his hands from the dining room, the cord just long enough for the phone to reach.

My mother steps out into the daylight and stands there, between my father who has started a conversation with someone on the phone, and the bands of light now softening, moving over them, as I squint up at my mother and hold my hand over the emptied glass. Iris holds her hand out to me. I am reluctant to take it, and she notices this and pulls back and collapses onto the chair behind her in the dining room.

Ryzu. Ryzu, She looks away from both of us as my father finishes the conversation and puts the receiver back in its cradle.

Iris, what did you do, how did this happen?

Her mouth opens, then goes slack, and it's like she's sleep-talking.

I don't remember the water falling it was falling and then I heard the strangest thing the birds crashing into the panes one after the other like broken pieces of wood when I went to them they were lying dead on the carpet and I tried—

Iris stopped as if pulled by an internal cord that had run out and motioned for my father to help her up. He led her into the pale glow of the kitchen and out onto the porch as I watched them go down the stairs, unevenly, sparingly, her arm in his, as if they had always known this day would come in perfect symmetry of body and gesture, like in the Picasso painting that had hung in my room throughout my childhood of the three figures by the sea: a man and woman and young boy, waiting it seemed for something to happen or trying to understand what just had happened. The sea in its blue quiet behind them, the three of them standing without word, near the blue plume of waves that had just started to land on shore as their bodies turned away, turned toward each other and stared at the circle of sand before their feet.

It was 4:30 on Sunday, June 9, 1968. I was 10 years old. My father was 58. My mother, at 51, had three years left to live.

TWENTY-THREE

Two months later, August, we left for Bethany Beach for the first and only time that summer on a morning that was overcast, looking like rain. The drive took about three hours in those days, as you headed out New York Avenue toward Route 50 and went through Salisbury, Maryland, staying on 50 until it became 13. As you got closer to the ocean the air changed, lightened by salt and the appearance of gulls flying low overhead. Bethany was a town from the New Testament, my mother had told me, the town where Lazarus had been raised from the dead by Jesus and was the beginning point of Christ's journey into Jerusalem on Palm Sunday.

My father and mother didn't speak much on the drive up, and I lay down on the back seat and watched the trees moving by as we made our way across Maryland into Delaware. At one point, my father stopped for a late breakfast and asked if I wanted to come in or stay in the car. I said, "I'll stay in the car."

"Suit yourself," my mother said, her newly changed bandages bright as flag cloth in the morning light, as they walked together into the diner.

We came into town before noon, drove past the Chief Little Owl totem pole at the end of Ocean Avenue, and up to the parking lot near the boardwalk. My father and mother got out of the car, went into one of the stores to ask for directions to the trailer park where we'd be staying. When they came out, my mother was wearing a new pair of sunglasses and my father was carrying a beach umbrella and red plastic bucket with a shovel.

"For you," my father said, putting the umbrella and bucket on the seat next to me. "So you have something to do on the beach with the other children."

My mother bent down to readjust the bandage on her leg. A small circle of brownish red ooze had formed in the middle of the gauze wrapped around her shin.

"We need to get to where we're going," my mother said.

"Yes, Iris," my father said.

We drove back out of town and down the highway the way we'd come in, for about five minutes, then pulled into the Sunny Day trailer park. After checking in at the office, we were shown to the trailer by a kid about my age, wearing overalls, barefoot, his face and arms tanned from the sun.

"We got some fans, if you need," the boy said.

"Yes," my mother said, "that would be useful. What do you think, Richard?"

My father looked into the trailer, fake pine paneling along one wall, a small fridge and sink at the other end, two small beds end to end.

"Can we have water?" my father asked.

"Bottled?"

"Yes."

"I'll see if we got any left. They go pretty fast."

"Where is the supermarket?" my father wanted to know.

"That's back down in Lewes," the boy said. "You just take the highway back out until you come to signs for Lewes. It's not that big, but it's got what you need."

My father sat on one of the beds while my mother stood in the doorway of the trailer.

"Okay, you folks let me know if you need anything else," the boy said and walked back across the gravel and sand parking lot into the office.

In the mornings my father left early to go for a swim, and my mother and I would remain in the trailer, lying together in the single bed underneath the window, the door open so that we could get some breeze going, the fan placed inside the door's opening and another fan going on the counter near the small stove on which, we were made to understand, only two of the four burners actually worked. Lying next to my mother, I'd hear the other families going about their day, moving off in cars to drive to Rehoboth or Dewey, and every so often the tabby cat that lived on the property would poke his head in and my mother would say, "Oh, look, he's come for a visit," her left leg resting on the pillow as her hips fell back heavily on the spring mattress when she pulled herself up.

The days went like that, the two of us in the trailer in the mornings, my father taking his walk into town for a paper, stopping on the way to have breakfast at the small beach restaurant on the boardwalk, while I was in charge of my mother, making sure she was comfortable, getting her bandages changed as needed. They'd stocked up on cigarettes and liquor before we left D.C. and the bottles rested on the counter underneath a small window that let in the morning light.

My mother didn't talk about what had happened back in June, so that it was as if her injuries were part of another time, another set of events: that no one noticed that she walked with a limp, that the discolored fluid oozing through the come with me to the beach, a Pan Am bag he used for the swimming pool slung over his right shoulder and two towels draped over his left. We crossed the highway and passed the observation towers that had been erected by the military during World War II to guard against German U-boats. Only a few other families were on the beach that morning and, after waiting a few minutes for my father to apply suntan lotion and lay his towel down on the sand, I went down to water and walked out into the sea until the water came up to my chest, then started swimming in a straight line away from shore. When I turned on my back, I could see my father standing on the shore, a newspaper in his right hand, his left raised in a half-wave toward me.

*

My mother lay her head back down and the light triangulated above us, the fan moving the humid still air in circles about us so that if I could feel driftwood on my palms, as the wind outside rose, and the skies suddenly turned blue grey, threatening thunderstorms.

Through the door I saw Annie, a girl from the next trailer over making her way among the trailers, her white bathing suit dusty and stained, and called to her.

"Oh not so loud, Andrew," my mother said, "my head is throbbing."

Annie went down beneath one of the trailers and her legs were dark as she bent down and pulled the tabby cat out from underneath and came over to our trailer and stood in the unscreened doorway.

"Hey," Annie said, small-voiced, looking in from the door,

"want to go down to the beach?" Her eyes were a delicate blue and her mouth had a slight tightness to it. A wisp of blonde hair swept across her right cheek and lingered there just above her mouth.

I moved my fingers along the waistband of my swim suit and heard my mother moving behind me, turning herself over on the bed. I saw her bandage was reddening and came near, and she said, "No I'm ok," and fell back to sleep.

Annie's face was pale and soft in the white sun as I turned, licorice scent on her breath.

"Ok, let's go, my mom said it was ok," I said.

When I turned back toward the interior of the trailer, my mother's body was still and unmoving on the bed and I thought *exactly like she was dead that's the thing she can't be but she already is.*

Annie had gone down to the edge of the trailer park and was waiting when I came up to her. She took my hand in hers, and we crossed over together, the white line going up the macadam like a cool band of water. As we walked, I imagined how the world would look divided like that, with the white line going up between forever, until you couldn't see it anymore. It came to me that Annie had come to find me, like Jordan before her had and Charles before him; that the world was filled with these meetings that seemed to occur by chance but were the places where we could slip through, find something out we hadn't understood before. Standing in the sun with Annie that day, I didn't care if I didn't know her well or she me; it was enough we could exist here together and go places, lingering in them the way the water would come up and divide wet shore from dry, and we could be standing in both at the same instant, both of us by the cool waters of the Atlantic, held by a silence we seemed to find with each other and no one else.

"You all right?" Annie asked, as we came to a stop just above one of the dunes beyond which we could hear the ocean waves hitting the shore at high tide.

"Yeah," I said, "I'm fine, just thinking."

"What about?"

"I'm thinking that I haven't got a lot of friends and it's nice to meet someone new."

Annie smiled, took my hand in hers, put it against her stomach, and said, "Well, now you got somebody, don't you?"

I smiled back at her. "Yeah, guess that's true."

I'd seen Annie and her mother and father and two brothers walking down to the beach together in the mornings, coming back around lunchtime, then sometimes she'd trail behind and stop in for a few minutes to say hello. I'd be sitting out front playing with a stray cat that had decided to make our trailer its new home, and we'd talk a bit about nothing at all, after which she'd go down the bend of the trailer park and disappear inside the white tin structure. I don't know that we cared about much at all, except getting down to the beach once a day at least and staying there for as long as we could. I could hardly have told her where or who I was, could hardly have said much that would have made sense at the time.

We were kids with time on our hands. "Too bored to live," we'd say to each other, "bored stiff," wanting to get out and do something and not sure what. Sometimes, in the evenings a group of kids would stand under the trailer park sign, the neon casting a soft glow into the evening, and they'd throw rocks across the highway that would fall into the tall grass that bordered the macadam. I'd look on from my place on the steps of our trailer, scared, but not scared enough to go inside, waiting for them to notice me, hoping they wouldn't see me there.

TWENTY-FOUR

When Annie came to our trailer that morning, I'd noticed how a layer of light flooded the inside of the trailer as I opened the door. My mother was sitting up on the bed behind me, motioning for me to go.

"Are you sure it's okay?" I said.

"Go, Andrew, I'll be fine," my mother said.

When I turned around, Annie was standing in the sun, her eyes half-shut from the brightness. I wanted to put my hand in Annie's hand and stroke the hair from her face, but I just stepped down the stairs in silence, feeling the rough sand on the soles of my feet, then the rough burn of the tar as we crossed the highway.

"We should go before the rain hits," I said.

"Rain?" Annie said. "Where'd you hear that. S'posed to be sunny all day, I heard."

"My father's radio," I said, "he listens every morning, WTOP AM."

"Oh, well, let's get going."

We walked along the beach in their direction for awhile, the storm cloud starting to roll in from the west as we did, and the waves turning darker green and heavier as they fell on the beach.

Annie pointed to one of the observation towers in the distance and said, "Looks like you were right, let's go inside, looks like a storm's coming," and we broke into a run together and I tried to keep up and screamed for her to stop and she laughed and the rain started to come down just as we got inside the large stone cylinder.

On the ground were discarded beer cans and charred wood and the torn remnants of a beach towel and we sat against the cylindrical wall and her feet were cut up from the run and I said, "Hey, you got cut."

"Yeah, it's ok," she said, "I usually do worse."

"Maybe you need some cream," I said, "I have some I use on my mother's foot and leg I can put some on when we go back."

She nodded and said, "Ok, maybe, we'll see."

We were quiet for a few minutes, then she said, "How'd your mom get those?" I didn't know how to answer or what it meant to try to tell it, start to tell what had happened to my mother, to all of us, then stop and begin all over again. *How'd she get those?* It was like the question didn't make sense, there was no possible answer or there were multiple answers, all of them right, all of them wrong. I didn't know what to say to Annie that made any sense of those events...

A cloud passed over us, then another, and my voice seemed to come from outside myself as if I were turning back the clock and the clock was running down too fast and I couldn't find the words to explain what had happened inside our house that night or the next morning when my father and I had found Iris.

"I don't really know," I started. "My mother was fine one afternoon when I left her to go to my dad's house, then the next...." I stopped, looked over at the sea, its waters rough and grey-green in the distance as it fell onto the shore.

"She did something to herself?" Annie asked.

"Yeah, kinda. I don't know, I think so."

I was looking for a way not to say it, as Annie played with a piece of Coke glass she'd found in the sand.

"You know," I said, "she was alone in the house, I should've been there but wasn't, and when my father and I came the next day, she was like that."

"Cut up, you mean?"

"Yeah, all cut up."

Annie threw the glass into the shadows behind us. "Rain's stopped," she said.

"Yeah, it has."

"She gonna be okay?"

I didn't speak for a time, then started to, stopped, my mind drifting back to what my mother might be doing in the trailer, where my father was, as if I needed to know at every moment where these people were, *if* they were.

"Who knows?" I said.

I realized sitting in the blue green hush of late afternoon, the heat storm passing over and blue skies emerging suddenly and the spitfire sound of engines on the highway, that what I had to say couldn't be told any other way, needed the breaks, the silences and incomplete parts that were mostly made up on the spot, that just telling it straight wasn't possible. It wasn't possible, I thought sitting on the sand with Annie, to know the difference between reality and its made-up versions. They fell together in a jumble of starts and finishes, half-said sentences that led to one part of the story, while another stayed silent, waiting to be picked up at some later date. My mother's life? My own life? Hers and mine? It was all corrupted, all broken like parts of a stone that had been chipped at so you could see the jagged marks but you couldn't find the other pieces that had been taken away. My hands weren't my hands, I wanted to say. My body's not my body. It's someone else's. Someone else is living here and did these things. Saw these things happen.

"Who knows?" I repeated, and Annie got up and walked to the tower entrance and put her hand out to catch the light coming back over the beach, sunlight just beginning to make its appearance again.

We walked back to the trailer park in silence, hand in hand like brother and sister. The next morning I would go down to the beach, and it would still be early, just after dawn, and the light hard and high on the shore, and the fishermen would be set up with their rods and reels and the lines would be going out far into the waves, and sometimes they'd catch one and it would come in flopping and heavy in the bright morning air. The bright fish flopping in the bright morning air, like a liturgy of movement and light. Summer was passing, the light steady and hard at the sea's edge. And behind me the sound of morning traffic moving up the highway.

TWENTY-FIVE

My father had moved back in with us from Quebec House in the early part of that summer, then moved out again after several weeks prior to our trip to Bethany Beach to the boarding house at the top of our street, a large mansion with columns rumored to have once been the home of Grover Cleveland, after whom Cleveland Park was named. "It's a temporary move," my mother had said, "just trying things out." I remember thinking *It's been tried and done, Christ, it's been done over and over again, and you both know it can't work with me here. That's the truth you both are keeping in front of you but acting as if I don't know.* There was no point in my trying to figure it out, like a large puzzle with half the pieces missing and some just not fitting anymore, they'd been forced into place so many times.

Richard came back to us a few times a week, though I was aware even with the infrequency of his visits that he was never far from us. "You can see him anytime you like," my mother said to me, and it was as if this permission were in itself to endure a kind of love or justification, to be part of this acknowledgment of separation that was an ongoing part of who we were as a family.

Sometimes I would spend the night in my father's room in the boarding house, sleeping on the pullout bed that he'd brought from our home. Downstairs I'd hear the other men who lived with my father as they finished their dinners, some moving outside for a smoke, others remaining down below to play cards, watch TV, drink.

"Can you sleep, Andy?" my father would say to me from

across the room, where he'd been reading his newspaper in the glow of the floor lamp he'd brought from home.

"I can sleep," I'd say, knowing as I did so that it would only be when he turned the light off and got into his bed that I'd be able to shut my eyes and drift off.

"You aren't sleeping, are you?" he'd ask.

"I was, but then the sound..."

He'd get up, close the door to the hallway, come back and sit near me on the bed.

"Better?"

I'd laugh, because it hardly made a difference.

"Better than what?"

"It will go quickly, go to sleep." He'd sit near me in his undershirt and unbuttoned trousers, his feet still in socks, and his suspenders fallen on either side of his torso.

Eventually, he'd turn in, shut the light off and get into his bed, the springs of his mattress rustling in the dark as he moved from side to side. I wondered if my father dreamed and, if so, what he dreamed of. He'd once told me that he often thought of his father in their last days together in Poland before the war and wondered what difference it might have made had he stayed in Warsaw when the Germans invaded, instead of fleeing with his brother to the east.

"What do you think would have happened?" I'd asked him.

"Who can say?" my father had said. "There were terrible things happening all at once very quickly. Who can say....but he would have known us for a little longer, that is perhaps the only thing that would have been different."

"But you might not have lived," I'd said.

"Yes, that is true." My father had paused for a moment,

then said, "And then there would have been no Iris, no America, no you."

"And no you either."

"No, you are right. No me either." I'd closed my eyes after he spoke these words and, as I fell asleep, kept hearing the sounds of the crickets and the dull quiet of the street outside our window that my father kept open, as if everything still and silent were meant to come inside our room.

One night I was startled awake by the sound of a car backfiring down the street, and saw my father had gone and went downstairs to find him. Everyone had gone back to their rooms except for Frank, a cook at Old Europe, a German restaurant on Wisconsin Avenue.

"Hey," I said, "have you seen my father?"

Frank looked over at me from the TV, the rest of the basement dark except for the flickering glow from the set. "No, kid, he went out. Can't sleep?"

"Where'd he go?" I said.

"Couldn't tell you. Saw him get in his car, though, about an hour ago. Didn't say where he was going." He paused, looked back over at the set, then said, "I'm sure he'll be back soon. You want something to eat? Can make you some eggs."

"No," I said, "It's okay. I'm not hungry. Thanks though."

I went back up to the room, passing on the way the rooms of the other men who shared lodgings with my father. The carpets smelled of mildew and the walls were yellowed and chipped where the paint had started to fade. I looked up and down the hallway, sat for a time at the staircase landing leading up to the third floor where the owner lived with his wife and two children, and across from me, through the window, I could see the trees motionless in the summer night and above them a few stars in the milky night sky.

When my father came back, I saw it was past two and his feet seemed unable to get their footing as he stumbled around our room.

"Daddy?" I said.

"*Proszę* ..."

"You okay?"

"*Proszę, jestem bardzo*—" he began, then corrected himself. "I am very tired Andy, go to sleep."

I watched him from underneath the covers, his belly heavy and swollen in the half-light, his trousers and underpants falling in a heap on the floor as he had shed his clothes. When he was out I came over to him and smelled alcohol on his breath as he began to snore. In the pocket of his pants I found some loose change and a piece of paper with a woman's name and phone number written on it: Elise EM3-4563. I put the paper back in his pocket and lay down on the bed with my father, fitting myself to his back as he turned over.

The next morning when I woke, the room was empty, and my father had gone. A note was taped to the door, "Be a good boy today with your mummy. See you soon, love Daddy."

TWENTY-SIX

As August bled into the fall and a new school year began, we saw each other as time allowed, no real plan to it. Those first days of sixth grade I spent with my mother; sometimes I'd visit my father up the street, sometimes spending the night, sometimes not. A few of the men I'd seen over the summer had moved out of the rooming house, as others had moved in. A group of Colombian men had taken the apartment on the top floor, sometimes sat outside nights after their work at one of the restaurants on Connecticut. My father didn't seem happy or unhappy living as he did, and when I asked him when he'd be moving back in with my mother and me, his face would take on a look that suggested there really was nothing to say.

One Saturday in late September, I rode my bike to my mother's house after spending the previous night with my father. The rain had come down hard that morning and the roads were wet and slick from the leaves as I came down the hill. When I opened the front door of our house, my mother was standing in the dining room, seemingly as I had left her the day. The light shone onto her through the panes when she stood up and came to the door and opened it. I was wearing a cloth coat, rubber soled shoes a size too large for me, no hat or gloves.

"Oh sweetie, you look cold," she said.

"No," I said, "I'm okay," and noticed that she'd spread newspaper out on the floor.

"What's that for?" I asked, pointing to the newspaper.

"Oh, the cats can't seem to get used to their new litter." It didn't make any sense, but I didn't press the matter.

Looking back at my mother, I remembered the song she used to sing to me at nighttime just before sleep, when I was five or six years old. "No bird can fly through these rooms without being caught." When I looked around the rooms I saw no birds flying, only the papers on the floor and some dishes on the table from her lunch and the typewriter beside them open on the table with a page of typescript emerging from the roller.

My mother took my coat and laid it on the sofa and took me into the kitchen and made hot tea with sugar and lemon and brought it back out to the dining room and sat with me at the table.

"How was your night with your father?" my mother asked.

"Nothing new," I said. "He went out early then came back. Are you going to Giant later?"

"Oh, I don't think so. We've got enough food here anyway, at least until next week." She drank from her cup and I watched the movement of the trees through the windows.

"You look tired, darling, like you didn't get enough sleep last night."

"No, I'm ok." I put my bag on the floor next to the sofa. "Daddy's taking me to the circus."

"Today?" she asked.

"Yeah, he thought it would be okay, since I don't have school tomorrow."

"I suppose so, yes. But you'll be back after, yes?"

"Do you want me to?"

My mother held her tea cup in her hand and straightened her skirt. "I think that would be best, don't you?"

"He was going to take me out for dinner after, so I don't know."

"Well, that's fine. Tell him you'll need to be back by ten."

"I think it's the big circus," I said, forgetting the name for a moment, "the one we saw last year. Ringling Barnum something...."

"Ringling Brothers Barnum and Bailey."

"Yeah, that's the one," I said.

"Don't say 'yeah,'" my mother said.

"Okay," I said.

"Okay, what?"

"Okay, mums."

"You should put your things away and get ready, if you're going to go to this circus," my mother said, having put down her tea cup and pulled a bottle from behind the drapes and poured some of the brown liquid into it.

"I've got time," I said.

"Suit yourself, but if he comes and you're not ready—"

"Fine," I said, took my bag upstairs to my room. The door to my father's bedroom was still shut, as it had been for weeks. I opened it and looked in and saw that my father's bed was newly made with fresh linens and that on the desk where he used to work a stack of books from the library rested up against the window.

I went back to my room and sat on my bed and remembered the year before when my father had taken me to the circus: how the elephants would walk the streets from where the circus train stopped near Capitol Hill and would continue through the city until they were gathered under the tents near Constitution Hall close to the White House. They shut down the streets and in some neighborhoods the children and their parents would come out to watch. I still remembered my father's eyes looking down at me as we raised our arms together in surprise as the elephants appeared at the edge of the avenue, walking in pairs, surrounded on either side by circus folks parading down the avenue with them.

When my father arrived later that afternoon, my mother had already had another several cups of her "tea," and her demeanor had shifted the way it did each day around this time.

"You could have asked me," my mother said, as my father helped me on with my coat.

My mother rested both her arms on the back of the sofa rest and looked first at him, then at me, and again back at him.

"It is possible, you know, to have communication with me about such things, even if you aren't living here."

"Of course, Iris."

"So the boy tells me you are going to the circus, but you don't bother to tell me?"

My father looked away, then said, "I saw nothing wrong, the boy wanted to go to the circus, I can take him, so—"

"Richard—"

"What, Iris?" I pulled myself away and into the half-light of the doorway.

"Not in front of the boy."

"He hears everything, what is it?"

My mother came across the room and brought her purse from beside the phone table. She opened it, motioned for him to look inside. "You see? Empty."

"I will take care of this, Iris."

"When? You said that last time."

"Soon. Let's go, Andy."

My mother followed us out onto the porch and shouted after us, "Jesus! For fucking Christ's sake, pay what you owe me."

Later my father would take my hand in his as we drove downtown for dinner and, with a pained look on this face, say, "Andy, I'm sorry you have to hear such things."

The streets were clear and the lights timed for the first time in a long while, as we drove across the city in the late afternoon and the wind came through the trees again and my face was softened by the light from each passing window.

A few nights later after I'd returned to my mother, my father met my mother and me at the corner of Porter and Connecticut. She'd told me he had something for her and I said, "What?" and she glanced over at me and said, "None of your business," and sprayed more *Aquanet* on her hair. We stood waiting for him in a pool of orange light in front of *Sav Mor* Pharmacy, my mother's hands were ungloved and pale in the light, as she lit a cigarette with one hand and held onto me with her other.

"It's getting chilly," my mother said, and pulled some lint off my sweater and looked up the avenue. "We agreed to seven, where the hell is he?" She steered me into the vestibule of the pharmacy.

When my father showed up about ten minutes later, my mother was just about ready to leave.

I said, "There he is," and she looked across the avenue at my father in the grey all-weather wool suit that he wore to work and said, "So he is. Stay here, Andy."

She smiled as he approached and said, "You could have been on time."

He knelt to give me a kiss on the cheek and said, "You are being a good boy with your mother?" I nodded, then looked off as another D.C. Transit bus pulled up to the stop in front of the drugstore.

My father pulled an envelope out of his vest pocket and handed it to my mother, who opened it, glanced inside, looked back at him and said, "Well, it will have to do for now. Electric's about to be cut off, so it's good you finally took care of this."

"Iris, not in front of Andy," my father said.

"Yes, god knows he shouldn't know what a cheapskate you are."

"Iris, please—"

"No, of course, because you'd rather he believe that you're actually holding up your end of the bargain and being a good father." My father withdrew and looked back at me as he started to cross the avenue to head back to his room at the boarding house.

"You know," my mother said to my father, "nothing's finalized yet, nothing's written in stone that you're moving back with us."

My father blew me a kiss then disappeared into the night.

On our way back up the hill toward our house, I asked my mother, "Is daddy moving back in with us?"

"Well, that's up to him," she said, "if he plays his cards right."

We got to the steps of our house, and my mother started to climb them, while I stood on the sidewalk and looked up the hill toward the boarding house.

"You want to go to him?" my mother said.

"No, mums, just looking," I said.

"Yes," she said, "I expect you were," and went up the next set of stairs onto the porch.

When she opened the front door I saw the light yellow like a small cut-out moon from inside the house and my mother's silhouette imprinted there.

TWENTY-SEVEN

"There was always something new," my father used to say, referring to his life with my mother. It was as if they'd formed a pact with one another, one in which separations and quarreling were as much part of the mix as being together in one place. I'd grown used to it, but the changes could still be startling, as one morning a few weeks after our meeting on Porter Street, I went down the corridor and saw my mother's door was closed and knocked and heard my father's voice inside, then hers.

"What is it, Andy?"

"Is daddy here?" I said and started to push open the door and there was stirring on the other side, as if they were hurriedly throwing clothes on.

"Be a good boy," my father said from inside the room, "and go downstairs and make some breakfast for yourself. Mummy and I will come down soon." I could hear the bed giving from the weight of their bodies and, a little later, the sounds of their movement, more steady and regular, as I sat downstairs at the kitchen table and waited for them to come down.

In mid-October of that year, my father was sent by Voice of America to cover the Olympic Games in Mexico City. I don't know how much my mother knew of what was happening in the country at the time, though there'd been reports on the evening news of the crack-down on protesters in the capitol, several people having been killed. Perhaps there had been a conversation between them, perhaps not. It's hard to picture my mother being protective of Richard, of wanting to keep him safe, in that period when he was regularly not with us, more absent than present. Their small renewals of affection, their itinerant efforts at family: some way or other, they seemed to say, we belong here, we will make this place our own.

Had there been others beside Richard in my mother's life? Once in the middle of an afternoon some months before, I had asked Iris if there had been other men, and she looked up at me from her book that she'd been reading in bed and laughed and said, "What kind of question is that to ask your mother?"

"I just wonder," I'd said, and she pulled the sheet down around her middle and put the book on her night table and said, "Well, what do you think?"

"I don't know, maybe."

She brushed a strand of hair off her face, smiled, and said, "Of course, dear, of course. Many, many men."

"Have I ever known any of them?"

"You mean have you met them?"

"Yes."

"Well, I don't know, dear...perhaps at some time, maybe one or two you've met. Why does it matter?"

"I don't know," I said, "I guess it doesn't." My mother had returned to reading her book. I remember Jordan's hands for no particular reason, how they'd rested on his knees when he was talking, the seemingly effortless way they moved through air, as he emphasized a point. There seemed, I realized sitting on my mother's bed that afternoon, no one reality any of us could share. There were always these shards, these dislocated pieces. You got them handed to you and had to figure out a way to make them whole again.

"You can't worry your head about such things," Iris sad, looking up from her book, "it's nothing you need to concern yourself with."

It was like a breeze coming up from the sea and the light stain of it on your skin, you can feel the breeze moving through and you know if you stand very still it will complete your body, the way wind and light complete a landscape, and if you stand still long enough it will all pass and nothing will have changed.

My mother and I were alone again, for one of the last extended periods of her life. Some of the letters my mother wrote to my father have survived, along with one of mine, written as I recall as a kind of "penance" for having misbehaved. Richard's letters to Iris, if indeed there were any, haven't survived. My mother's tone in these letters is one of kid-like fondness and, occasionally, passionate concern. They are documents of daily life written as factual accounting. If emotions were revealed at all, they were conveyed through the language of declarative statements. Much of my mother's correspondence with my father concerns financial matters, and it seems clear from her letters that money played a critical role in what they had to say to one another, not least for the fact that throughout their married lives they seem not to have had much money to spare. For whom money was more important is hard to say.

The first letter is dated, Friday, October 12, 1968, the opening day of the games, and was typed on blue aerogramme stationery and postmarked "Washington, D.C. October 13 AM":

Darling:

Your insurance came this morning – no letter for you, but from the Perpetual came a letter saying that if we pay now the cost is $10,000. They didn't say how much I save if I pay now, but that our payments would finish in 9-10 years' time! I supposed we only stand to save $1,000 and this over a period of 9-10 years, but even so, I think our plan is a good one especially when you never know what might happen on the Stock Exchange. Incidentally, there are some lectures given by members of the Stock Exchange (Ferris & another firm) at the Chevy Chase Community Center beginning next Thursday at 9:30 a.m. and I am going to them. There are about 5 lectures and the total cost is $2.00, so it's worth it, and I can drop Andy, too. (Today Geico is 81 ½).

Just for the heck of it, I phoned Friends Sibley School – it costs $1250 per year!

Andy had diarrhea this morning – not too bad, but he went to school one hour later and I gave him a note for Mrs. Ferman.

I went to the doctor and he said I looked fine. I told him I had had pains in my right chest, but examined me and said there was nothing to worry about, it was just a muscular ache. I was relieved because I thought he might operate for cancer! In fact, I was so relieved I forgot to ask him about my medical check-up – this I will ask Monday week, when is my next appointment (& I am having the flu shot!).

We both miss you very much and we wonder how you are in Mexico. Is the apartment nice, and how is the food? Are you being kept very busy? It is too bad we won't hear you on the radio.

We had a letter from the Boy Scouts saying that there

is a meeting of boys and parents on Wednesday next in the National Presbyterian Church at Nebraska Ave. at 8 p.m., so I'll take Andy to join if the location is okay. Incidentally, Chevy Chase Community Centre is still in the programming stage of roller skating, and if they do have these activities, they will be at the old Bureau of Standards, as you know; but I'll have to double check.

Yesterday, we went to bed at 9:30 p.m., but neither of us were sleepy. Saturday night there's a good TV program at 9:00 and at 11:15 they have *War and Peace*, though we'll probably be too sleepy to watch it.

I'll leave the other side of this letter for Andy to finish when he comes back from school. He wanted me to wait for any Giant shopping although actually I don't need to buy anything.

The GEICO insurance installment invoice came today and I paid it.

Tomorrow, it's supposed to be nice weather – it's horrid today – so maybe we'll go down to Sloan's for some new furniture for the house. We're going to do the house this weekend, and I'll just sort out Andy's clothes, launder his summer things and put them away. There's no point in doing laundry today – nothing would dry – it's so damp.

I just got back from Safeway – I was going to buy potatoes; they were 10 lbs. for 69¢ and 20 lbs. for 79¢ (isn't that ridiculous?) so I decided to wait for Andy. Anyway, I bought oysters, the first, and I thought how you would like them! The flowers are still beautiful and it was lovely of you to buy them for me. In relation to what they cost and what they mean to me, I'm surprised you never thought of that.

On the other side of the aerogramme, I wrote to my father:

> Dear Daddy,
>
> Last night I woke up and found that I had to go to the bathroom. I had a bit of a stomach ache and I had to go four more times before I was relieved of this. Now I am feeling a lot better and we both had a great big dinner consisting of: oysters, boiled beef, carrots and potatoes. Soon if I am a good little boy I shall receive some apricots. We probably will be going to bed in another hour. GOOD NIGHT MR. MOSSIN.
>
> Your
> Son
> Andy
>
> Love and kisses from both of us. xxxxxxxxxxxx See you later alligator.

With the exception of my mother's slight rebuke in the closing sentences, my mother's letter reads as a newsy, sometimes loving account filled with concerns over money and small details from our days. There is none of the anger that I recalled from so much of their time together nor anything like the anger that would fill her letters in the coming few years, as if she were moving from storm to storm, barely able to see her way through.

Iris's letter a week later, five days before the closing ceremonies in Mexico City would happen, was also written by hand and reads:

Tuesday Oct 22

Darling:

Your p.c. came for Andy today together with your letter for both of us. Perhaps tomorrow I'll get a letter from you addressed to me.

Yesterday the termite man came & left a report – all okay.

I haven't had to cash a check yet but I might have to before you come back. I bought $100 Mutual Dynamics Group for Andy in his name (no income tax on it) & this takes care of the $70 you owed him. GEICO is still up as you probably know, but I'm selling Chamberlain while it is 16 ½ - 17 ½ (I paid 14 ¾) because it will drop if there is a real peace move.

Did I tell you I got 2 bottles of your Scotts hair tonic & a Scope gargle? We also bought on sale 2 plastic trash cans for only $1.99 each & 2 laundry baskets for only $1.00 (I didn't need but it was the 1¢ sale!)

Andy hasn't been a good boy but I've told him he has got to change & he has promised to turn over a new leaf! I learned that he has been expelled from his French class 5 times! And this doesn't count expulsion from other classes. He is sure he is going to get another bad behavior report from school – this come in 3 weeks time. So I've told him to pull his socks up between now & 3 weeks. Last weekend he spent the <u>whole</u> time reading Magellan's explorations & writing an essay for the extra credit. He is doing a lot of homework and there is no time for TV. We don't even watch the Olympics although he gave his news report in school yesterday from an editorial of *The Washington Post* on the 2 black U.S. members of the Olympics who were expelled, which I wrote for him

It's bright lovely weather here but cool.

The animals have settled down together in harmony, tho still disunity at feeding time.

Your days seem terribly hectic & I hope your health isn't suffering. Will you be recompensed for the weekends and the extra overtime you are putting in?

Love,

Iris

The final letter from this period, written by hand in the same blue-green ink on ruled three-ring-punch paper and dated "Tuesday evening," reads as follows:

Darling:

This evening a lady from VOA called to say that her boss had a message for me from you – that you were so extremely busy you were not able to write to me. As a matter of fact, I had realized that! I know the Olympics start early & end late & that you are getting interviews with people / also having to go to the Embassy. I hope you're not overdoing things especially in that climate & altitude. It's not worth risking your health.

The lady said they were all listening to your broadcasts which were tremendously interesting.

Andrew will be telling you of Princess's disappearance yesterday. I had phone call from a young girl about 4:30 p.m. to say they had our dog & that she was 3225 Woodley Road.

I drove there with Andy & we just couldn't the locate the 3200 block at all until I discovered that 3225 was the

Chinese Embassy & took up the whole block. As a matter of fact, it's almost like a park – the house nestles way back in the ground. I drove back by way of the Eaton school.

A letter came from the Mexican government tourist office to acknowledge my letter & to say they were disappointed you couldn't visit Mexico, but hoped we would come another year. Very nice letter!

Nothing has happened & no interesting mail for you.

Andy doesn't want to join Boy Scouts. He is allowed to ride his bike to school on Friday to get it registered.

As I'm going to attend the stock market lectures beginning Thursday at Chevy Chase library I'll be driving him to school.

The weather is warm & damp here with a heavy fog.

We cleaned the house last weekend, but we haven't done anything to the back garden, primarily because the tomatoes are still green so we can't put weed killer down until they are ready for picking.

The animals still play together & "rough house" but not with malice.

Here is an unused stamp – you can lick it on the back of the envelope gummy part so it will stick.

I waited for the mailman Wed a.m. in case there might be anything from you, but there only a letter from Polish Daily which I enclose.

Benebunes
Iris

My mother seemed to have run out of things to say, her paragraphs shortened to a sentence or two. And her letter—one that began with a plaintive response to the woman from Voice of America who called to inform her that my father had no time to write—ends with a similarly fraught note about the lack of mail.

My mother's mentions of me seem oddly out of place in these letters that want to push toward other matters, other issues of concern, yet don't. Her voice reads now as an effort to keep things light, write as if nothing has happened or were happening. One sentence following another, the activities of our days listed in order, nothing possessed of more importance than anything else. I come into these letters as "Andy" or "Andrew," strangely in place, misplaced, disregarded and held in view, even as I'm part of the list of things done, things accomplished, warnings over behavior mixed with admonitions over a future that was awaiting us. And "Richard," the man to whom these letters were addressed? He's there, missed for what he didn't write, didn't send onto my mother. An unused stamp sent back for a letter that wouldn't arrive.

TWENTY-EIGHT

Iris and I began sharing a darkened house those weeks my father was away, the grey curtains pulled across from late morning until sundown because the sunlight hurt my mother's eyes. I was her "little man," she told me, there was nothing we couldn't do together. In the mornings I was taken to Phoebe Hearst Elementary by her or walked on my own, the day starting off bright and sunny and warm, so that by the time I reached the top of our block, I'd removed my sweater. Once it fell into the street and when I reached school, I realized it was gone and feared what my mother would say when I returned home without it, but on the walk back home it was still there, blue with green buttons, resting atop a hedge where someone had placed it as they'd been passing by.

The streets lay under canopies of elms and maples, and as I walked I collected leaves and brought them home to my mother, these and the last flowers of the season, hydrangeas that were still in bloom, marigolds and fall roses.

"Where'd you get these," my mother would ask.

"Oh, they were growing wild by the side of the street," I'd say, and she'd know immediately that I was lying, though the smile in her eyes told me it didn't really matter. Sometimes she'd make a face in mock anger, indicating this would be our little secret. She'd then put the flowers on the tin table in the kitchen, where she prepared a vase of cool tap water mixed with aspirin to keep the flowers alive longer.

The days seemed brittle and soft at the same time. We would go into the garden and pick the remaining ripened tomatoes or rake the leaves that had fallen the night before into neat piles in the back yard. One afternoon, while kneeling in the garden bed, I saw a bright silver wire sticking out of the ground and pulled at it until an eye glasses frame emerged, and I held it up to the light and saw that it was the pair I'd lost when I was seven. I brought it in to show my mother who had gone upstairs. When she turned, she made an odd face. Her mouth seemed to have caved in on itself, and she held up her dentures and laughed and said it was a terrible thing but true that she was better off without them in, after which we went back downstairs again.

When I showed my mother the frames, she said, "Well, it's a good thing you found them. We can't keep buying me new frames year after year."

I laughed and said I didn't think it would be every year but perhaps we could donate this pair to the collection at the public library. She took them from me and placed them on the kitchen counter and walked away. Later, I could hear her moving a glass from behind the drapes. Then it was quiet again, and she came back and said we should go to Giant, there was probably a sale of something.

As I got ready to go, I could hear her sitting on the sofa and taking a swig from her bottle and then putting it back just as I appeared in the doorway with my coat on. We'd be heading up the hill on Connecticut to the Giant Food at Van Ness that had opened only three years before. My mother looked over at me and shot me a glance that said "not yet," and I went out to the garden and saw that the leaves had nearly covered the entire yard and knew I would be raking that weekend, probably taking down the fence that protected the tomatoes as well as the stakes that held the now-faded plants upright. I walked back inside and sat on the chair in the kitchen and played with the stuff that was in the table drawer, matches and a Bic pen, and wrote my name inside the drawer in script like I'd been taught at school. When I looked up at the clock it was 4:30, and the light was starting to change. In the other room I could hear the drapes being pulled back into place, and the light steady and sharply reduced as I came in to get her.

*

I don't know when my father returned to us, sometime around the end of October or early November. He was just there one morning, as I was getting ready for school, his jacket on the chair in the kitchen as he prepared breakfast for himself before heading off to work. Iris and Richard didn't discuss these changes with me beforehand; they just happened and it was always as if the light in a room had suddenly been lowered, then turned off, and when it returned a table or chair had been moved and a figure who'd been absent was now sitting in the once vacant chair.

You must stay with Iris, Richard would say to me repeatedly during each of these removals followed by a return. *You must be good to her so you can have nice times together.* There was a sort of paralysis to my father's phrases, they came so regularly repeated throughout those years I heard them as spacers between events, not as anything real in and of themselves. Often Richard would appear to me in my dreams, threaded through images of flying birds and water, this image of my father, standing at the top of the staircase, starting his descent. It was like he had moved from one step to the other, but was never able to descend, not fully. And if I turned my head one inch to the right or left, it was if the image of him disappeared. There was no way to retrieve what it was that had gone or what it was that came and went again.

Iris had relaxed into our solitude that was also our common time, as if she had reconciled herself to a life with one or the other of us, never both at the same time. "Perhaps this is a better way" she would say to me, "just being here with each other the way we are. Nothing more or less. Just to be here the way we are."

What couldn't we know? What couldn't we do? My mother walked down the street and walked back up it again. Daylight shifted to evening. She would be walking, I believed, the same direction she had always walked and I could follow her. The game we'd play would be hide and seek. "Come find me," she would say, "I'll hide and you come find me." As if we were two children playing together. As if everything came down to this single game of chance and discovery...

"You have to find me," she would say, as I watched her disappear into a side alley. "I'm going, here I go," she would say, and her grey cloth coat would disappear like the sail of a small boat disappearing from the horizon.

When I woke, Richard and Iris would both be gone, their twin voices still and motionless above me in the empty house.

TWENTY-NINE

Our walks those fall afternoons would begin the same way as the pre-evening cold set in and the light had started to fade. "Where to?" my mother would invariably ask, even as she would already know, and she would nod slowly and rise from the sofa and walk a bit unsteadily toward me with her hand outstretched as if reaching for something. She'd pull her cloth coat from the closet and put one arm through one sleeve, the other arm through the other sleeve, and with her coat on she would stand ready before the door, waiting for me.

"Ready?"

"Ready," I'd say. I would get the wire shopping cart from its place at the side of the house, and we would walk down Ordway toward Connecticut Avenue, crossing the street just before reaching the bottom of the hill, my hand moving across the steel bars *one two three four five six* of the railing that separated the upper wall from the street and shops below.

The route was always the same. We turned and passed the florist and dry cleaners and Chik'n'Bucket, I could see the light as it formed over the spires and abutments of the Kennedy Warren apartments, the late sun reflecting from the windows like blue stones on a red background. My mother held my hand as we crossed the avenue and moved past the apartment buildings and trees on either side of us, the beige and red brick buildings familiar as any I had known, with their elaborate balconies and entryways, so that I wondered who lived there and what their daily lives must be like, each building proposing itself as a world all its own, estranged and isolate in its way, and at the same time linked in some fabulous way to an interior understanding of the world my mother and I shared.

She and I would often not speak for blocks at a time, until she noticed something that aroused her curiosity and made her stop.

"What do you think," she would say, "who lives there in that place?"

"A man and his three children," I might offer, and she would smile and say, "Oh, perhaps, or maybe just strangers, a boarding house, it looks kind of rundown, don't you think?"

We'd pass another house that had seen better years as well, and the grass would be growing high on the property, obscuring the cement porch and steps leading up to it. My mother would run her hands across the grass and smile inwardly, and I would notice that her fingernails had traces of soil under them from our gardening the day before and her wrists were thin and pale and bare as she ran her hand across the grass spears and walked carefully beside the stone wall that was at hip level as we passed. The tall ships, she said to me once, sail in the white sea, and it had been years since I had thought of the ships, their masts arrayed in the white light of Potomac, how her hand drew me to her body, as if we could set sail together, return to England or Greece or…and find homeland again, she said it was the purpose of all longing to find anchor again, to become native to one's land again, and what happiness we had on earth she said came to us from our ties to landscape, air, light, sun….The tall ships in passing, let us pass with them….

And the point of our trip would quickly seem to have no point other than to do something, take a journey together late in the day, the belief persistent that we had no place else to be, that our time was ours alone, that we could squander it at will, make what we wanted of a day, an afternoon, minutes passing without notice.

Descending by elevator to the lower level entrance of the Giant, my mother and I would usually head immediately to the damaged and reduced cans section, many of them missing their labels, their prices written in bold black marker across the exposed tin. 79¢. 49¢. 85¢. We didn't know what was in most of the cans, but it didn't matter, my mother said, there was no doubt something we could use, green beans or peas or sometimes Campbell's soup. Half the time I think my mother bought these to appease my desire for us to come away from our shopping trip burdened down with groceries, though I also knew that my mother had little money to spend on anything and this was a way to stock up for the cold days ahead when she didn't want to drive and walking was difficult for her from the recurring pain down her right leg and shin from the skin grafts of a summer ago.

"Mums can you walk? Is it ok?" I'd say and she would look over at me and smile.

"Oh yes, Andy, it's fine, let's go, I'm fine."

As we rounded the last street before returning home she would lean against the brick side of the apartment building at the corner of Porter and Connecticut. Young kids would be coming out of the Seven Eleven with their cold drinks, and a few would stand against the side of the building by the bus stop and wait for the H4 or H2 to take them down the hill. Sometimes one of them would step forward and ask my mother if she had a light, and she would sometimes respond, sometimes not.

Then there would be those evenings when she would ask me to wait for her and go in and come out with a bottle of Michelob in a brown paper bag and would swig from it as we made our way together through the back alley behind Yenching Palace restaurant and the fire station where once when I was eight I'd gone in the middle of the day and found no one inside and had stared up the brass pole in the center and stood on the rubber mat for I don't know how long before going back out into the bright light of day.

When we went down the bakery aisle at Giant, my mother would look again for the bins of reduced, day-old bread, cakes, and doughnuts. Sometimes, there would be still fresh loaves of pumpernickel or rye on sale, but most days the good bread had already been sold and there would be only a few passable loaves left, which my mother would squeeze with her swollen fingers before placing one in our basket.

"Are we poor, mums?" I asked her one afternoon, as we made our way through the grocery store aisle.

"God no. But we have to be careful." Her face seemed without emotion as she spoke, surprising given what I knew of my parents' money troubles.

"Because we don't have enough money now that daddy's away again?"

"Because we have to be careful. Your father—" She didn't complete the thought, as we left the store and made our way back down the avenue toward home.

THIRTY

Many nights that fall when my father was still away, the skies opened up in a blaze of color: fuchsia mixed with strands of poppy and crimson. "Red sky at morning, sailors take warning. Red sky at night, sailor's delight," my mother would say. The days seemed to hold a new promise in them, as if this latest separation were performing some necessary healing of our family.

Together at dusk, my mother and I went through the neighborhood near our house searching for kindling. Each evening we left our house with that common goal in mind: to load up on twigs and branches that had fallen into the street from a rainstorm or been brought down in a heavy wind. The skies would be near dark, the "gloaming time" she would call it, and we'd start in the same way each evening, with half-steps down the cement stairs of our front porch, angling to the left as we came to the sidewalk and heading up Ordway until we'd passed 29th Street, moving steadily up toward Reno, which we'd cross, sometimes hurriedly, sometimes slowly, her pace steady with mine, slow steps into the next block, pausing every so often to bend down and grab at a branch or group of branches and putting them in the bags we'd brought with us.

My mother wore a silk scarf tied tightly around her chin, and I would often still be wearing shorts from summer and my work boots bought at Kaufman's on sale for $6.99. My hair was cut in the same military crew cut I'd had since I was 5, and the clothes I wore had lasted me several seasons already, some bought together with my father years before at a mall in northern Virginia about an hour's drive from our house.

One night in early October my mother and I passed the corner house on 29th Street and saw a pile of newly cut logs from an oak that had been sawed down. My mother passed back and forth in front of the house, inspecting the logs as she did so, looking into the yard and waiting for someone to come out, but no one did.

"C'mon, Andy," she said, "let's ask," and I went up the walk with her and my mother knocked on the heavy wood door and we stood on the porch a few minutes waiting for someone to come out.

A woman looking to be in her early 40's, wearing blue jeans and a white jumper came down the hallway and opened the door, and my mother told her we were from up the street and were looking for firewood and wondered if…and the woman said, "Oh sure, help yourself, we can't possibly use that much, take as much as you want."

"Thank you so much, you're very kind," my mother said, kneeling down for a piece of kindling, her cloth coat opening for a moment, the last button falling away, and my mother's hand reaching for it, putting it back in her pocket, as she continued to pick up kindling.

"I'm Eva. This is my daughter Miranda. Want to come in for a minute? I've got something on the stove." Eva stepped back from the doorway, as Miranda moved herself closer into the doorway's frame.

"No thank you, perhaps another time," my mother said. Miranda peered at me through the doorway and I could see she was wearing jean shorts and a t-shirt and I didn't understand—it was so cold—how she wasn't cold too.

Looking past my mother, Miranda said to me, "Hey, you should come over some time," so that for a moment it was the two of us standing there looking at one another in the silence that followed, and I murmured something about the weekend, maybe if I didn't have homework, and my mother looked over at me then back toward Eva, who said, "Well, you've been very kind, I'll come down with Andy tomorrow with our wheel barrow, and we'll collect the wood."

"Did you think she was nice?" I asked my mother as we moved back up the street toward home.

"Nice enough," she said, "you can't always be sure with people when you first meet them, but yes. Nice."

As we moved up the darkened street near the corner where years ago I'd spotted my father staggering, seeming unable to get his balance as he moved up the hill toward home, I returned to the smell of cooked food from inside their home, the vegetable broth and warm noodles on the counter in the kitchen. My mother's hand clutched mine as we moved up the stairs to the front of our house and down the street I saw that Eva and her daughter were moving toward the avenue together and as they walked they bumped hips into each other and laughed together so that I could hear them as my mother shut the door of our house and turned on the hall light and went up to bed.

It was dinnertime, but I knew there wouldn't be dinner tonight. Iris would lie down for awhile and maybe get up and maybe not and if I was hungry I could come back down for something. There would be something in the fridge, and I'd sit at the aluminum table in our kitchen and eat and listen for the sound of the buses passing on the avenue or our neighbors next door, moving through their house as they often did late into the night.

THIRTY-ONE

Miranda and I started visiting with each other during the weekdays after school, sometimes on the weekends when her parents were out and Miranda was alone in the house and I could visit for hours at a time until my mother yelled my name out across the alley so that I could hear her from Miranda's bedroom.

"You really got to go?" she'd say.

"Yeah, I think so."

"You sure? Can't you stay for dinner? I know my mom wouldn't mind."

I'd look over at her and pull on my dungarees that had gotten pulled off in one of the games we played like a ritual that we'd invented: dice thrown on the floor, loser had to take a piece of clothing off until one of us was naked. "Doing dirty stuff," Miranda called it, and I said, "Okay, but if I get cold I'm going under the blankets," and she'd smile, say, "Yeah, 'course, stupid, and I'll climb in with you."

Most afternoons, I'd leave Miranda in her room with her magazines, some books thrown on the floor, the sheets falling to the floor as I left the bed and it would be nearly 4 o'clock in the middle of a November day and there was no other sound on earth I could hear but the low wind coming through the trees as I returned up the block to the house where my mother awaited my return.

During school days my mother asked me to be home by dinnertime but otherwise seemed unconcerned about what I might be doing or where I might be, not noticing when I returned later in the evening. My mother and father had settled into their separate lives, with their nights spent apart in their separate, adjoining bedrooms. Sometimes when I woke in the mornings my father had already left—or never come home, it was never clear—and as night came and he still hadn't returned, I would ask my mother if my father was coming home that night.

"I have no idea," Iris would say, and turn back to her book and glass of gin or Scotch. There were limits to what she would or could say, my mother's response suggested, as if we had come to this agreement together *not* to say, *not* to offer reasons, just accept the days as they came.

"This world is not my home, I'm just a passing through," went the old Gospel song, and each of our days and nights that fall seemed confirmation of that. My mother slowly disappeared from view, as had my father, both gone in the wink of an eye, present and not present at the same time. After a period of initial closeness, my mother withdrew from me into her own world. As for me, I no longer knew my place in it, if I ever had, though I understood with each passing day that wherever I was meant little other than that I was somewhere, alone or not, there or not there.

Often, I would come back from Miranda's house to find my mother sitting on the sofa in the living room, the evening dark surrounding her, as she sat without lights on.

She'd look up when I came into the room, flick the ash from her cigarette, take another drag, look toward the door, as if someone else were coming, as if she'd mistaken me for that someone and now had disappointment moving across her face in a slow flexion of her jaw muscles.

"You already ate?" she'd ask.

"I had something, not much," I'd say.

"Well, there's food, go make yourself something if you're hungry."

"Yes, mums."

I'd get whatever was left in the fridge—some slices of white bread, American cheese, left-over chicken—and make myself a plate and sit at the white tin table in the kitchen, as my mother sat in the dark in the living room. Eventually, I'd go upstairs and listen for the sounds of my father's keys in the lock. Some nights I never heard him, only knew he might be home when I passed his bedroom door in the morning and saw that it was shut. But I couldn't ever be sure, not really.

"You want to come over?" Miranda's voice on the phone.

"Sure."

"I got some new stuff for us."

"What's that?"

"You'll see," she said, tightness in the back of my throat as I put the receiver down and walked down the hill to Miranda's house. The girl down the street *that little girl you won't leave alone* my mother called her. Sometimes Jordan came back to me, Annie from Bethany, the lost people of my world. I'd conjure them up until I was almost in tears, an ache in my chest as I realized I'd never see them again. *Jordan is dead now*, I said. *Annie is dead and gone now. These are not people I'll ever know again.* There was a rhythm to the loss, like a tightrope that kept looping back and back, hand over hand, you could watch the rope all day long, tightening and lengthening, stretched between sets of invisible hands. Still light as you lay under it and watch it pass over you. *Let their bodies pass over you*, I said, *let them all pass.*

I learned from Miranda that her mother had come over from Hungary just before Miranda was born. Miranda's father, Mihály, had stayed in Hungary after the Russian invasion in 1956, keeping his job as a steelworker for a while before escaping the country the following year for France. There'd been talk early on of his joining Eva and Miranda in the U.S., but nothing ever came of it and eventually the couple divorced. By then Eva had moved with her daughter to the Outer Banks in North Carolina where she worked for a realtor and managed rental properties up and down the Outer Banks, from Nags Head down to Hatteras. In the off-season, Miranda and her mother took trips up north, visiting with folks Eva had become acquainted with through her work. On one of those trips to D.C., Eva met George, a store manager for the local Giant Foods. George was in his 50's and apparently regarded Eva as a "good catch," a young woman in her early 30's who seemed happy in his company. The two were married when Miranda turned seven and they moved into George's house on 29th Street. George had rented out the second floor bedroom to his meat department manager, but when George proposed to Eva he told Carl he'd have to find other lodgings. Eva got a job waitressing, first at a local bar in the Dupont Circle area of D.C., then was able to get part time work in a dental office up Connecticut near Florida Avenue. The hours were okay, she'd thought, and she'd have more time to spend with Miranda. It didn't turn out that way, as most days Eva ended up heading back downtown to meet up with her old friends she'd gotten to know in the D.C. area over the years and sometimes wouldn't come home until well past dinner time.

There wasn't much to say about George, Miranda told

me one day after we'd laid ourselves out on the bed in her bedroom, amid the stacks of teen fashion magazines she liked to look through.

I asked her if George was good to her.

Miranda nodded, said, "Mostly."

"Not always?" I said.

"He can be mean, I guess," Miranda said, chewing on the rubber eraser tip of a pencil.

"Like how?"

"Just mean. Like he'll walk in and see that stuff's not been put away in the kitchen and come up screaming that I haven't done shit, he's been working all day and what the hell have I been doing."

I told her it could be the same at my house, though it was usually my mother doing the yelling.

"He ever try to do stuff with you?" I said, not sure why I was asking though it seemed reasonable to wonder.

"Once," she said. She'd grabbed a tennis ball from under the bed and her hands had started tossing it left to right from one hand to the other.

"What'd he do?"

Miranda paused, took a breath, said, "Okay, no one knows about this, not even my mom, okay?"

"Yeah, sure," I said.

She held the tennis ball still in her right hand and stroked at its surface with her pinky finger.

"I was ten, just after my birthday. So this is, like, three years ago. He comes back from work and my mom's still out. I don't say anything to him when he comes back, can tell he's in a bad mood, something at work, he doesn't say, just goes in the kitchen and opens up a can of beer. I go back up to my room, just staying out of his way, and he comes up, smiles at me, says I'm getting to be a pretty big girl. I said, 'yeah, guess so,' and watched him out the corner of my eye as he sat down on the bed next to me and stroked my hair back. 'What's up?' I said to him, but he kept stroking my hair and telling me it was like my mom's, he always liked to stroke my mom's hair that way and she must like it because she never asked him to stop."

I knew where she was going and reached out for her hand. "No, it's okay."

She continued with her story. "His hands smell of raw fish, like he'd been working the fish counter at the store. Somehow his hand moves down from my head and over my chest and he held it there. I didn't say anything, just sat still as his hand moved up and down. He started to unbutton my blouse and I pushed his hand away. I could see his thing had gotten bigger in his pants and I stood up and started putting some of my clothes away. He didn't seem to think anything of it, just said, 'What do you think we'll do for dinner, any word when your mom's coming home?' I shook my head, said, 'Dunno, she didn't say,' watched him get up with a heavy sigh, eventually walking back downstairs."

"How come you never told your mom?" I asked.

"What's she gonna do? Divorce him? Not likely. Chances are she'd have said it was just a misunderstanding."

"Do you think that's what it was?"

Miranda stared off for a moment, then said, "Yeah, the kind that happens all the time."

I told her what had happened with Jordan at Wild Goose Farm and she said, "Least he was close to your age."

"Yeah," I said, "I suppose that's right."

"And he didn't hurt you."

"No, I guess not."

"It happens, you know. You just gotta be careful all the time, you never know when someone's gonna try something."

"Yeah," I said, wondering how one knew.

THIRTY-TWO

By the spring I was spending several afternoons and some evenings each week with Miranda and her mom and stepdad. Weekend days came and I would head down the hill from my house to meet Miranda for breakfast, then stay for lunch and when dinnertime came around, I'd often be invited to stay as well. It was like it had become my real home, so that Miranda even kept a change of clothes for me in her room.

"You're obsessed with that girl," my mother would say to me one afternoon in February.

"No, she's just nice."

"You could make other friends, or at least try to."

I'd shrug and say, "It doesn't matter, at least I have one friend who cares."

One day later that spring my mother tried to stop me from going over, said it was too much and she was getting tired of having to go down the hill to find me.

"I'm going, I don't care," I said.

Iris picked up an ashtray from the table and threw it in my direction. When it smashed into pieces against the back of the bookcase, she said, "Go on, then, get out. Don't come back."

"Okay," I said, "I won't."

After that, my mother more or less gave up on trying to control where I went or when I came back. Sometimes she would stop by to check in and if Eva was home she'd say, "Oh, they're around here somewhere, you want me to send him back on up?" and I would hear my mother's voice, "No, it's fine, just tell him I'll leave the key under the ledge in case I'm out."

"Sure," Eva would say, "I'll be sure to let him know."

In the afternoons with both her mother and stepdad gone, Eva and I had the place to ourselves. We'd move from room to room, starting in the kitchen and heading back into the dining room with its drop leaf table and chairs that didn't match and ending up in Eva's bedroom upstairs. One day Eva took me into her mom and stepdad's room and pulled a set of cards out that George kept in a dresser drawer.

"You want to take a look?" Miranda said.

"Yeah, what are they?"

"Like nothing you've ever seen," she said and lay the cards out on the carpet. The images on the cards were of people doing things to one another. The men were nondescript, heavy, looking bored and tired as they leaned over or lay on top of women whose eyes seemed neither open nor closed, tranquilized almost, not tranquil but waiting and not waiting at the same moment. As Miranda lay them out on the carpet before me, I tried to see each figure in the pictures in some way familiar, a pause in the loop of time as they spoke to one another in the pictures, were saying words I couldn't hear, one of them halfway on his back and his mouth caught in this expression that was someway between a grimace and a cry of pain.

"What do you think?" Miranda said, watching me for my reaction.

"It's like they're playing some sort of game, I guess. Kinda weird. Can't really tell what they're doing."

"I mean, do you want to try to do some of this stuff?"

I thought about what she was asking me and it didn't make sense at first.

"You mean you want us to get in these positions? They look like they're playing Twister or something," I said.

Miranda smiled, took my hand. "It's okay, we don't have to. Just thought it would be something we could try."

Her hands smelled of talcum powder and lemons as she stroked my cheek and kissed it. "You think?" she said.

I picked up one of the cards from the floor. A man had pulled down a woman's jeans so that they were wrapped around her ankles and he was mounting her from behind.

"Do you like this one?" I said.

"Sure," she said. "Where do you want to do it?"

"On the floor?"

She turned and unbuttoned her pants and stepped out of them and took her underpants off and threw them next to her jeans. I pulled my shorts and underpants down and got behind her and she said, "You have to put it inside me."

"I'm not sure I can," I said.

"Sure you can, let me show you," and she directed me into her, then turned to face me.

"It's ok," she said.

"I want to," I said. "I just...."

"Yeah," she said, "I know."

"I do want to."

Miranda had put her pants back on and was sitting on the bed, while I stood in front of her with my shorts still around my ankles. I thought I heard my mother calling me from our house but it was quiet and the light started to shift and I saw that Miranda had started to tear up.

"What?" I said. "What is it?"

"Nothing," she said.

"It's something."

"It doesn't matter." She gathered up the cards into her hands and replaced them in the box. "You're sweet," she said.

"Do you want me to go?" I said, not sure how to read her movements in the light.

Miranda looked up and her eyes squinted half-closed as if she were trying to focus in hard sunlight. "Naw," she said, "it's okay. Let's go down and watch some TV."

I pulled my shorts back up and felt a breeze through the open window and looked out over 29th Street and saw that it was getting near dinnertime and wondered where my mother was, what she was doing, if she was still awake or already passed out from drink.

And it came to me that Miranda was asking me for something, I didn't know what exactly, something familiar and new at the same time. I began to understand that whatever we got to know of each other would never be real knowing, we couldn't get there, we never would.

My body felt tired, worn out from the day and all the days before this one. I looked over at Miranda and saw the light flicker across her face from the TV screen, blond strands of hair falling across her right cheek. Outside there was a hint of evening coming across the sky, the way the light shifted to shadow and the trees and houses all took on the appearance of unreal things from another world. And I remembered a passage from the Book of Job that my mother had read to me often, so that I'd more or less memorized it: "But where shall wisdom be found? And where is the place of understanding? Mortals do not know the way to it. The deep says, 'It is not with me.' It cannot be gotten for gold, and silver cannot be weighed out as its price. It cannot be valued in the gold of Ophir, in precious onyx or sapphire. Gold and glass cannot equal it, nor can it be exchanged for jewels of fine gold…It is hidden from the eyes of all living, and concealed from the birds of the air."

*

The day came to a close. When I returned home, our house was cold, the heat turned down to 60 degrees in the middle of a cold spring. My mother was sometimes out when I returned, I didn't know where she'd gone to or when she'd be back, and the sun had fallen so that the day seemed like it had cracked in two, and in one part I was still living while in another I had already left this world for another.

I would go to my room and lay on my bed, and wait for my mother to return and when she did I would sometimes go down and sit with her as she made dinner. It would be quiet that way between us, few words exchanged if any, and when I got up to leave the table my mother wouldn't say anything, wouldn't try to stop me as I made my way back upstairs to my bedroom. Sometimes I'd turn on the clock radio that I'd found in the garbage of a neighbor's house several months before and would listen to the top 40 AM station as I looked up into the tree limbs and noticed the few stars just above, marking the sky like bits of chalk on a blue-black background

THIRTY-THREE

Miranda and I met for the rest of the school year into the late days of spring. I didn't understand much of what we did, but it felt good to have Miranda take me in as she did. I once asked her whether it mattered to her that I was only 11, and she responded, "Not really, I think of you like my little brother, my kid brother," and I said, "Yeah, it's like that, I guess," even as it struck me that most brothers and sisters probably didn't do the things we did.

Throughout this time, my mother seemed both oblivious to and resentful of the time I was spending away from her and with Miranda. "You're all wrapped up in her," Iris would sometimes say, "Why don't you spend the day here for a change?" But nothing ever came of those offers. I didn't have a response for her, shielded by all that had passed between us and now couldn't find a way into plain light of day. She stared over at me from her place on the sofa and said, "Well, suit yourself, can't say I didn't try,"

"Okay," I'd say, "so can I go?"

"It's up to you," my mother would say, a look of diffident hurt crossing her face.

Her newspaper spread out on the coffee table in front of her, I'd wait five, maybe ten, minutes, before slowly walking to the door and heading down the steps to the street. When I turned around, I would see the silhouette of my mother in the pane of the living room window, her eyes watching me go.

Once my mother found a pair of Miranda's underpants

in my drawer and asked me, "Whose are these?" and I lied and told her I'd found them in the trash, and she turned from me and left them there, though the next day when I went to find them they were gone.

Nothing I did seemed to matter, even as my mother spent mornings and afternoons writing notes to herself about my behavior: lying and disobedience, stealing, refusing to listen to her—as if she needed to document my acts to convince herself of what was happening. *There's only one truth, Andrew, one way of looking at the world that's right and true. You either hold that in your heart or you don't. Nothing I can say will make a difference until you believe that.*

Miranda had come by for me one afternoon and my mother answered the door and I heard from the stairs as she told her that I couldn't come out, I'd been punished. I couldn't hear much else of the conversation, just the sound of Miranda going back down the steps and walking down the street toward home.

As the spring passed into early summer, I saw less and less of Miranda. She'd appear at the back door of her house, her eyes peering out into the back alley, and when she saw me coming she'd close the door quickly, as if she'd gone into hiding. I didn't really understand what had happened, then one day in early May came by and knocked and when Miranda came to the door, I said, "Hey, you wanna do something?"

She glanced over at the apartment building just behind their house and said, "Naw, can't, gotta wait for my mom to get home."

"Oh," I said. "Everything okay?"

"Yeah," Miranda said, still eyeing the building, "everything's fine."

"So you gonna be around this weekend?" I asked.

She looked directly at me for a moment, then away again. "You know," she said, "I don't know."

"Yeah."

"Probably not."

"Did I do something wrong?" I asked after a long silence.

"Hey," she said, "what do you think?"

"I think you don't want to hang out anymore."

There was another long silence and her right hand came up to her face, as she pushed a strand of blonde hair out of her eyes, and she looked toward me, then away, as if there was no place she'd rather have been than in that doorway.

"It's okay," I said, "I get it. See you around, I guess."

"Yeah, for sure," Miranda said, and closed the door firmly shut, as I moved back into the alleyway and walked back up the hill toward my mother's house.

THIRTY-FOUR

A woman's hands had lifted me once, had brought me close to her body, though I couldn't remember their texture, their scent, even as they often seemed nearer and more real to me than the hands of those whose touch I experienced in my daily life. I had been caught, held captive, it seemed to me, then released....but where? I often thought of the myth of Judas who was born to Cyboread. Warned in a dream that her son would prove ruinous to his people, she placed the boy in a pine box and released him into the sea. The waves cast him onto the island of Iscariot where the childless queen raised him as her son. Later, the royal couple had a son of their own and Judas, feeling slighted by the presence of his foster-brother, killed him. Judas's betrayal of Jesus years later was foretold by his birth, or so I came to understand the meaning of this story long after I first heard it.

"Why did you and my father bring me to this country?" I once asked Iris at the end of a long day we'd spent together. A shocked expression came over her face.

"What kind of question is that?" she said.

"Why did you bring me here if you didn't want to have a child."

"We wanted a child, very much. We didn't know how it would be or how difficult."

"Then why did you adopt if you weren't ready to take care of someone?"

"Darling..." she began and her voice trailed off. "I couldn't conceive, that was why, and your father wanted a child, very much, and so you...."

And she stopped and her dishrag fell onto the floor and I picked it up and gave it back to her. I could hear her begin to try as she turned back toward the sink and next door the neighbors had returned from work and there were the sounds from next door of dinner being made and down the next house the new tenants who had been away for a month were in their yard preparing a barbecue on their grill. And it was like a tri-fold world we were in, so that I could see at any one moment the other worlds folded into ours, those we weren't part of nor ever could be, and sometimes it was as if we really could have been placed anywhere and none of it would have been any different and what happened next or what had happened before were only reflections, nothing more, of some other state of being that we would never reach, never know.

When my mother turned, her face was pale and soft and she said almost in a whisper, "What do you want me to say, Andrew. What do you want me to say?" Her hands rested on the sink ledge and she pulled the strands of cat hair off her skirt and let them fall to the floor, and held up her hands and shrugged, and I understood that this was all she seemed able to say or offer, and I moved into the corridor and went up the stairs to my room and took off my clothes and prepared for bed in the full daylight.

It was 5:30 p.m. on a Wednesday in June. We were entering another season. My mother's wounds had faded, so that all you could see were the shiny parts of her skin where the doctors had performed skin grafts. A large knot the size of a half-dollar appeared in the middle of her right shin, and her right heel was half gone where they'd had to remove the scarred flesh.

My father and mother had separated again, after a short spell of trying out a return to living under one roof.

"Where's daddy going?" I asked my mother, noticing the boxes that had not long ago been unpacked loaded up again and sitting on the floor outside my father's bedroom.

"Oh, just down the street," she said

"Why? Why's he leaving again?"

"No reason," my mother said, "just for a little while."

"There's got to be a reason," I insisted.

"No, dear, there doesn't have to be one at all. Go on, go outside and play until it's over."

My father appeared in the hallway, just as my mother had closed her bedroom door. I came over to him and watched as he leaned down to pick up a box and carry it downstairs.

"You want any help?" I asked.

"No, Andy. Be a good boy, just go play by yourself for a little while, like your mummy said."

"Okay, daddy," I said, as I followed him down the stairs and out to his car sitting in front of our house, its back trunk door open in the afternoon light.

When I returned home later that afternoon, my father's car was gone. Outside on the porch, my mother had placed a bowl of grapes and a glass of gin.

She came out when she heard me come up the stairs and said, "Well, here we are, just the two of us."

I nodded and walked into the house.

THIRTY-FIVE

Sometime during the spring of 1969 my father came back to live on what promised to be a more permanent basis with Iris and me. I don't remember how or when, but he returned and life resumed some sort of normalcy. Though, of course, it was the normalcy of separations and adjustments and repeated breaks that represented whatever "real" life we shared as a family. I looked for signs of regularity in the small things to find them again and again gone missing, then sharpened by what they once had meant in another context, as if moving from one part of a hillside to another you discover the light is different, the shadows more prominent, yet there's no escaping the transitory nature of each space you enter.

All I knew was that my father had reappeared with some regularity in our lives, was there in the mornings, most nights came home to my mother and me, so that it seemed as if the long period of separation might finally have come to an end. If I knew as well that this wasn't likely, that more changes would occur, more separations and partings, I kept such thinking off to the side, ready to play make-believe again in the face of circumstances I had no control over.

"Your father is here," my mother would suddenly announce, the day having just begun, and I would nod, move into the corridor, catch a glimpse of him through the open door of his bedroom, then make my way downstairs. It made no difference or it made all the difference. I could never decide which. But the pieces that had been broken over and over again never could never really be put together again.

Not really. Not for any period of time that made sense. So, my mother spent her days in bed, came down for meals—or not—reading steadily through the afternoons and evenings and nights, sometimes books I'd brought her from the public library, often from our bookcases in the living room.

"The war" was always with us those days, even when it wasn't talked about directly. The war was the Vietnam War, which by the summer of that year had been going for nearly a decade. Walter Cronkite and Harry Reasoner were on the evening news programs, and the sound of Lyndon Johnson's voice announcing another troop increase or another bombing campaign in the North. My mother, sometimes standing in the center of the living room, would shout at the TV through the broadcasts, "Goddamned fucking America. What a fucking joke this country is." If my father happened to be near, he wouldn't say anything, often just move off toward the kitchen so that I'd hear him opening the fridge and closing, again and again, taking things out, putting them on the counter, while Iris spat and cursed at the TV. He knew that trying to calm her was useless, would likely only anger her more, so would wait for the storm to pass then rejoin her in the living room. Often I'd go back upstairs to my room and listen to the sounds of the jets passing overhead as they did often in those days and the late evening bird calls in the trees and wait as well for my mother to have returned to herself or one self I felt safer being around.

Richard seemed to have little to say in response to Iris's outbursts, even as his work at Voice of America, as I only understood years later, was to provide the official U.S. position on the war and much else to his Polish audiences back in Poland. There didn't seem room for any other viewpoint, and my father gave up trying to have a reasonable conversation with my mother about a topic that, if they didn't quite agree on, seemed also beside the point. My mother spoke of America as a foreign country, even as she'd been a citizen of it for more than 15 years and my father nearly as long. Her reading in those days included books like *Vietnam, Inside Story of a Guerilla War; The Smaller Dragon: A Political History of Vietnam;* and *Last Reflections on a War,* titles I would recall years later when I read Frances Fitzgerald's history of the war, *Fire in the Lake,* in college and remembered the books I'd seen on Iris's night stand. This wasn't her land, not her place, she would say, and day after day I came to understand it wasn't supposed to be mine either, that I wasn't its child, one of its people, but something else, something or someone detached from homeland of any kind. Stateless before I knew the meaning of that word.

"We have to get out of this country," Iris began saying on an almost daily basis, "I can't stand it anymore. We have to leave." I had little idea what she meant, since I couldn't imagine anywhere we could go that would be any different. But Iris was committed to finding a way to return to Europe, if not Great Britain, for some part of the summer. Over the next several weeks, she began looking into the possibility of our traveling abroad. One day sometime around the beginning of May, a few weeks after my birthday, my mother announced that she'd found us a deal on a flight to the island of Mallorca, off the coast of Spain. From my bedroom, I heard her talking things over with my father, then silence as he took it in, finally saying something about needing to find someone to take care of the house, the cats, the garden.

"Oh for Christ's sake," my mother said, "we're not going to stay here because we can't find someone to take care of things."

"Let me see," my father said, "let me see about taking time off." Iris had stopped working altogether by that point, other than the occasional freelance article she still sent off to the Indian daily that seemed interested in my mother's views on American politics, especially in light of the expanding war in Vietnam. It wasn't clear to me if they were still taking her stories, but with the war news coming in as it did my mother seemed to have regained some of her prior energy for news writing.

"Such a trip will be very expensive, Iris," my father said. "We will need to plan carefully." Given my mother's frugalness with expenses and the ongoing cycle of expenses from my parents' on again-off again living situations, I didn't understand where the money for this journey overseas would be coming from, but it wasn't my place to ask.

It was like a cage coming down around us, I thought. Another cage we'd have to live in, as we traveled away together. I recalled our time on the Delaware coast two summers before when I'd been left to care for my mother, while my father spent most of his time away from us. I saw something like that emerging again, even as it might mean a period of change, a rolling back of responsibilities and fixture, perhaps even a kind of freedom.

My mother seemed near-frantic in her desire to return to Europe, while my father showed little enthusiasm for the trip.

"What will we do there for so long?" my father wanted to know.

"Oh Jesus," my mother said. "We'll visit the sights. We'll show Andy what the world looks like. He has no idea. And we'll be away from this country. Isn't that enough?"

"And you think he is ready for this?"

"We won't know until we find out," my mother replied.

"Then you can make the plans," my father said. "Do what you want. Just tell me when you have made the arrangements and I will tell you what we can afford."

By this time, my father had returned more or less full time to living with my mother, though he still kept his small apartment just down Connecticut overlooking Rock Creek Park. I visited him there occasionally, sometimes had dinner with him, never much more than hot dogs cooked in salty water and some coleslaw he'd picked up at the Safeway. I didn't understand why we were going to Europe when neither my father nor mother seemed able to stay long in each other's presence nor why my father chose to keep a second place to which he'd sometimes return in the course of an evening.

"You and mums going to live in one place again soon," I'd ask him.

"I think so, yes, but much is up to Iris."

"I see," I said, not that I did or ever would understand.

THIRTY-SIX

The nights and days of late spring passed one after the other, folded into summer. We spoke less and less about traveling away, more about where we would stay when we got there. "It will be a house by the sea...." my mother said to me one night. "There will be bougainvillea and the air will smell of lemons and honey. You will have your own room overlooking the ocean and every night you will go to sleep with the sound of the waves pounding at the shore." She showed me a map of Europe from an old issue of *National Geographic* and I could see Spain shaded pale green and next to it Portugal in bright orange and the strip of blue Mediterranean passing beneath. Across the water and on the other side of Italy and underneath the yellow landmass of Turkey was Greece, shaded in intricate brown swirls, as if to denote the country's mountainous regions...I wondered if we would be going there, how far it was to Greece from Spain. My mother's finger hovered over the island of Mallorca, hovering off to the west of the mainland, a floating emblem of green surrounded by pale blue.

I heard little else as I drifted off to sleep, only the sound of the Mediterranean, hitting the rocks of a beach I remembered from a lifetime ago.

We left Washington on a warm summer morning from Dulles International Airport, flying across the Atlantic to Spain on Iberia Airlines. My mother had wanted us to fly British Airways but there were apparently no good bookings available. The flight over was long, memorable mostly for its silences, the rudimentary way we didn't speak to one another, my father and I sitting together it seemed for the entire flight without exchanging a word, while my mother appeared at an odd angle from us, complacent, quieted, buried in her book. There were descriptions of cities, valleys, parks, her restlessness absorbed in the syntax of her guidebook. As I looked over I could see the pages falling one after the other in perfect order, the cathedrals and museums of the island where we were going marked off in light pencil in the margins. My mother's fingers smoothing over the words and images in felt-like strips of shadow.

On the flight I was mistaken for a Spanish boy by a woman in the seat behind us who spoke to me in Spanish, the language seeming at once familiar to me and unrecognizable: "¿De donde eres?" "Where are you from." I turned around and shook my head. "I don't understand," I said. I noticed that around her neck the woman wore a small gold cross that hung from a thin gold chain, her hair stiffened by hair spray.

"¿Tu eres Americano?"

"Yes," I said. "American."

We landed at Palma de Mallorca airport on a Sunday in July in the middle of a heat wave, the area around the airport deserted as we made our way into town, through the dust-encrusted blooms of poppies by the roadside, and the dust-enfolded fields falling back of tile-roofed houses we passed along the way. A few children stood at the road's edge watching our car pass en route to the tourist beaches and hotels. We passed house after house, their red tile roofs clay dark in the mid-afternoon sun. The town seemed uninhabited, as our taxi sped up the hill toward our hotel. We came around a bend in the road to pass a woman walking down the hill, her body clothed entirely in black, as she carried what looked like a shopping bag in her right hand. My mother nudged me as we passed her, though it wasn't clear what she meant for me to notice. A few roosters lingered by the road's edge, their red-feathered bodies collating like small weary fans smoothed out against a dusty surface. The ground flattened out, dust flakes simmering in the hot July sun, so that when we arrived at our hotel our bodies were covered in dust from the roads and sweat that coated us in an uneven sheen. My father lifted his shirt from his skin, as my mother removed the light sweater she'd worn on the plane, revealing her pale arms. Inside the hotel lobby, a group of school children stood together and sang what we later learned was a traditional Mallorcan folk song:

> A Mallorca hi ha una dama
> Que és hermosa com el sol
> Te la caballera rosa
> I llarga fins els talons.
>
> La mare la pentinava
> Amb una pinteta d'or
> Valgam Deu, Aina Maria
> Robadora del meu cor.
>
> La padrina els hi lligava
> Amb un floc de set colors
> S'estimat la se mirava
> Amb els seus ulls robadors
> Valgam Deu, Aina Maria
> Robadora del meu cor.

When they finished, the children ran off into the afternoon sun, while my father made arrangements for our rooms with the hotel desk staff. In halting Spanish, he asked for two rooms—"una cama de matrimonio y una con dos camas individuales"—one king bed and one room with two single beds—and when the desk clerk asked, "Dos habitaciones, ¿sí?" he responded, "Si, dos habitaciones."

That evening, my mother told me something of the history of the city, that the capital of Mallorca, Palma, was founded as a Roman camp called Palmaria on the remains of a Talaiotic settlement. The turbulent history of the city saw it subject to several Vandal sackings during the fall of the Western Roman Empire. It was later re-conquered by the Byzantines, colonized by the Moors who called it *Medina Mayurqa*, and finally established by James I of Aragon.

As my mother talked, I put my head down on the bed and heard the sounds of families in the swimming pool below, and I fell asleep to the music of a folk singer who played late into the night, his songs blending in my head into one long song of unutterable beauty, the singer's voice rising and falling in my semi-conscious state like ancient ballad from my childhood, something just at the edge of memory.

*

"Tortilla de huevos con jamón, por favor." At every meal I asked the waiter to bring me the same dish: omelet with ham and cheese. My father and mother ate sea bass, scorpion, pickerel, octopus grilled and brought to the table on a plate with rice and fresh vegetables. I drank red wine mixed with water in juice glasses, while my father had a tall glass of beer and my mother red wine, followed by Scotch or gin later in the evening. During the days, we swam in the hotel pool that overlooked a cove surrounded by high rock formations. The Badia de Palma lay below, blue-green in the morning light.

Everyone we met seemed to be from someplace else, though we were the only Americans, as far as I could tell. A father and his two daughters, Victoria and Emily, from Scotland were staying in the hotel, along with a South African family. Their son, Alec, and I became friends during the weeks we stayed at the hotel, often going down to the beach together to swim in the Mediterranean. Sometimes we waited for Victoria and Emily to come down and join us. They would sit with us for awhile, speaking in accents that made it hard at first for me to understand them.

"We shan't stay long, you know," one of them, Victoria, said to us one night. "We can't, really can't. Besides it's past your bedtime. Shouldn't you both be back with your mum and dad?" Victoria's voice rose into the perfumed night air, while behind us the sound of music came from the lobby below.

"Anthony," she said addressing me in the name I'd given her. "Your mum will be worried, won't she? And how about you, Alec, you the ring leader here?"

Alec smiled mischievously, but said nothing.

Both Victoria and Emily laughed as they swung out of view, heading down the steps past the pool to the rocky shore below.

"You think we should follow them?" I said to Alec.

"No, they'd be mad at us. Besides, our folks must wonder where we are."

I watched as Alec went ahead of me back toward the hotel and I turned and looked back across the moonlit sea and heard the waves coming in, then the sounds of conversations coming from the balconies above. Our room was dark, though I couldn't be sure if that meant that my father and mother were asleep, or if they were perhaps in the hotel bar together.

"I think I'll catch a swim," I yelled out to Alec as he stood in the doorway of the lobby and looked back over toward me.

"Yeah?"

"Yeah," I said and stood at the pool's edge lit from within by bright lights that gave the water a deep blue-green shimmer. I dove into the water, not coming up for air until I'd swum three lengths under the surface, the water warm and thick-scented from the bougainvillea, the blue light from underneath enveloping my body.

One evening Alec and I came down the path from the pool to find Victoria and Emily with two of the young waiters from the hotel, their bodies shadowed near the terrace and locked in embrace beneath a rock overhang. One of the girls had taken off her blouse and the light darkened the crease below her right breast. Her arms were slender and pale and she pulled the boy down to her and moved her hand toward his crotch. He was standing, then lying atop her on the stones and earth and her sister and the other young man had disappeared, though we could hear their voices through the darkness from our hiding place on the path.

"Do they see us?" Alec asked.

"No, they can't." His face was sharp, pale in the light from the pool lamps, his mouth held in a tight smile.

"Do you think we will see them tomorrow?"
"Maybe, but they don't seem so interested in us."
"I guess not."

When we returned to the pool, my father and mother had closed the blinds of their hotel room. Slivers of light from within played against the side wall. A few gulls flew above through the darkness, their wings forming shadows on the blue stone surface of the patio wall.

*

My father mostly left us alone; it wasn't clear where he went during the days, sometimes with a driver, sometimes on foot into town. Regardless, he came back most evenings to have dinner with us in the hotel dining room. He'd wear his freshly pressed white linen trousers and matching shirt...the smell of his aftershave lingering on him as he passed behind me.

In the afternoons while my father was away, I visited my mother's room when she was resting during the long hours of high heat and humidity. When I entered the room, it would be dark, the drapes pulled across the window overlooking the patio, the air heavy, still sweet from the bougainvillea blooming on the trellis outside. Plates from room service would be stacked next to the bed and, on the nightstand, my mother's glass of wine, half-finished, would sit near a travel guide.

"Keep the drapes closed," she would say to me. "It's stifling in here, but the sun only makes it hotter." Her body was covered in sweat and, when I sat on the bed next to her, I was nearly overcome by the odor.

"You can do something for me," she said. "Here, put this on my forehead. Use some of the tiger balm as well." She handed me a moist face cloth and a small plastic container of balm, and I placed it on her sweat-shiny forehead and stroked her temples, applying the tiger balm with my fingertips as I did so.

Her hands would sometimes accompany and guide mine, as they brought the face cloth up to her forehead, then fall back to rest again on the white sheets. On the index finger of her right hand she wore a slender gold band. Her left hand was bare except for the bracelet she wore: silver with an engraved set of initials.

"You have no idea," she would say, referring to the heat or the pain she was experiencing from another bad headache. They came daily, sometimes twice or three times a day, and each time my mother would retreat for hours to her room, sometimes not emerging until late in the evening. My father seemed not to notice or he had by that time assumed that Iris wouldn't want his care, so it was left up to me to help as I could.

Sometimes, my mother would pull me close to her body, her breath heavy with the combined aroma of cigarette and wine, and it would remind me of nights back home when I'd come to her room after seeing light still on late into the night and she'd asked me to rest with her awhile. *Just put your head here little one put your head here so that your mother can rest it's what I need just rest. Put your hand over mine yes like that and leave it there.* Her hands moving across the fabric, smoothing over the folds. I would linger there, amid the sweat-dusk scents of her ankles and feet, and kneel beside her and wait for her to pull back the covers and bring me into the bed with her.

My darling my little dove just for a little while just come in for a little while.

The books would fall to the floor as she pressed me into her. "Here, baby, here you want mummy to hold you, baby...."

I wouldn't look into her eyes or say a word. I would press my head onto her belly and lay flat in my swim shorts and towel and listen to the sounds of the fan, as it circulated the warm air above our bodies, the folds of my mother's nightdress damp and heavy on her body.

We stayed in Mallorca for two weeks. Days went by; the children from the nearby village came by in the mornings and sang their songs to the tourists and were given some money sometimes by those willing to spare a few pesos, then disappeared again. My mother lay down each afternoon with a headache that she would tell me were really migraines, but headache was easier to say. I would sometimes play table tennis with my father, before he left in early afternoon for his own activities.

One day he came back from town with a small donkey made of wood and attached by elastic string to a wooden base. When you pressed the underneath part of the base, the donkey collapsed onto all fours. I sat for minutes at a time, watching the donkey fold up, then rise again, fold up and rise. A woman came over to me one day, her body sharp and wet from the pool, and saw me playing with my mechanical donkey and said, "Oh, my goodness, where on earth did you get that?"

I shook my head, feigning a lack of English. She walked

away after a minute of staring down at me, her body moving between the palms toward the hotel lobby before disappearing inside the hotel.

Victoria and Emily left soon after our night on the beach and I would never see them again. Alec and his family left soon after. The days passed without event or seeming boundary between them, one after the other. I asked my mother when we would be returning home, and she nodded, "Soon," and disappeared again into her room.

I walked along the beach in the afternoons, the steps leading down covered in shells and sand. A few families rested under umbrellas, while above, from the hotel pool came the shouts and screams of the children visiting with their parents. I walked along the thin outline of shore, until I reached a rocky incline, then turned back again, the hotel a stucco construct of glass and red tile raised on the horizon.

A man in his fifties approaches me one day, sat down, and pulled out a newspaper. He said to me, "¿Puedes leer inglés?"

His voice was cracked, filial, like his words had always been part of my vocabulary.

I stared up at him from my place on the shore, the sand hot and wet between my toes. "I'm eleven years old," I told him. "My name is Andres. Andrew."

Tengo once años. Mi nombre es Andrés. Andrés.

The man smiled, took out an orange from his backpack, peeled off the skin, pulled off a section and held it out for me.

"No, gracias," I said. He waved away my hand, offered it to me again.

"Gracias," I said, taking the wedge of orange and biting

off a piece, before throwing the other section on the sand behind me, as the man turned his gaze toward the sea.

"Cuanto tiempo llevas aqui?"

"No lo sé," I said.

"¿Qué?"

"No español."

He stuck another piece of orange in his mouth, then said, "Ah, si. Americano?"

"Si."

"You are here with parents?"

"Si, with my mother and father."

"¿Te gusta Mallorca? You like Mallorca?"

"Yes," I said, "it's beautiful."

"Pero…" he said, searching for the words in English. "But very poor."

His eyes turned away from me toward a family moving into the water together, as his hand grasped his pack and took out a local newspaper.

"Adiós, chico," he said, and wandered toward an empty area of shade near the overhanging rocks ledge.

"Adiós," I said and made my way up the steps back to the hotel. When I came up to the pool, the children and their parents had disappeared. Lunchtime had come and gone. A few older couples sat with their drinks at poolside, while a box turtle appeared underneath a potted palm and disappeared into the undergrowth at the pool's edge.

My father would return by the evening meal; my mother would join him, and I would sit somewhere in between, a last piece of omelet left on my plate. They would tell me it was the custom to eat late, get up later, spend the days doing nothing. When they left me to go their separate ways, I sat beneath a canopy of bright stars that emerged like points of light on black glass. Another day was coming, another one after that, without end.

THIRTY-SEVEN

"When you've known death," Iris said to me one summer evening of our last year together in 1971, "you're not afraid, you know what it is, and it never leaves your side. There is no direction, no way back or forward, you just realize it's there, part of you, as if you had never known anything else." My mother's voice shone out of a ring of shadows in those days that we spent more or less together, more or less apart in ways that had become, for all their unpredictability, familiar, understandable, altogether normal.

At the beginning of June, my father traveled to Poland for the first time since he and Iris had emigrated to America. The day he left he came upstairs to my room and said to me, "You and mummy will have to be good to one another, Andrew. You must understand that she needs you to be good, to do what she asks."

I had turned thirteen that April, had gotten used to the pattern of things, the separations that went unexplained or, when explained, were somehow meant to be about my cooperating with Iris.

"Yeah," I said. "Whatever."

"Andrew."

"I get it: you want us to have a good time while you're gone. I get it."

"Andrew, please," my father said in that tone of voice that always signaled his inability to be heard—by my mother or me.

I looked away, out the window, saw the tree limbs bending

in a slight wind, got transfixed on the light the way it could hold branch and squares of color in the same position.

"Ok," I said.

"You will try?"

"I'll try."

"Kiss kiss?"

"Sure," I said, as my father leaned down and kissed me with wet lips on both cheeks. "Have a good trip. Bring me back something."

Richard smiled, turned and an hour later a cab took him to the airport.

My mother was sitting downstairs, drink in hand, and I came down and said, "Should we start making dinner?"

I could see by her body's movement where she was, didn't need her to say anything, it was pretty clear.

"Did your father talk to you?"

"Yeah," I said.

"Don't say 'yeah.' Yes."

"Yes."

"And?"

"And what?"

"And did you understand him?"

"Yeah," I said, "I understood."

My mother glanced up at me and said, "You can fucking get out with that attitude. Just fucking get out of my house."

"Okay," I said, and walked back upstairs and packed my knapsack with some extra clothes, my reading glasses, and a couple of books from my bookshelf.

When I went out the back door, I heard my mother come behind me and slam it shut and lock it.

"Good," I said to myself and walked into the late afternoon

light. I didn't know where I was going, didn't know how long I'd be gone, but the air had this quality to it, like it was drenched in magnolia light, and I wasn't afraid of anything and saw where I was going and was headed there.

One night followed another. I slept out in the back yard of our house, saw the stars come out above the tree limbs that formed a network of branches across the sky and I could see that my mother had gone to bed, left no lights on, doors locked front and back, no key under the porch ledge. I got a tarp we kept under the back porch and pulled it over myself on the chaise lounge that had half its nylon bands coming undone and sometime in the middle of the night woke cold and bug-bitten and turned over and saw from the dark skies that it was still a long way until morning.

I eventually made it back into the house, after first finding both doors still locked, front and back, and walking around until late morning when I saw the front door open and the figure of my mother emerge. Her body froze there when she saw me, following which she went back into the house and left the door open. I came up the steps and opened the door and moved past her as she stood in the living room, her body turned away from me as I entered the room. Without saying a word to her, I went to my room, where I stayed until evening before going back out again.

THIRTY-EIGHT

April 1967

Dear Richard:

I ask of you one thing: never to stop owing us both, as my husband and as the father of our son, Andrew,

Love
Iris

Benetunes

Our last summer together, my mother kept a journal on a drugstore tablet, recording there each of my acts of theft, betrayal, deception, escape from home. She wandered into the evenings looking for me, going house to house, sometimes lingering at the corner of 29th Street and Ordway to stand there, facing neither backward nor forward, but somehow sideways, parallel to the line of trees that spanned one side of the street to the other, until she moved against the weight of her own body it seemed, up toward the houses on Highland Place, her legs pale in the low light of evening. I could watch her from behind cars, moving as she moved, just a bit behind her.

Sometimes, I could tell she knew I was following her. But it didn't matter. She would keep moving to the next house, the door would open, our neighbors would appear, my mother would ask if I'd been seen, a few moments lingering there on the porch in the quiet white summer light, and then she'd say "Thank you, no, thank you, you are very kind," and come back down the stairs to the street. I played a game in my head, *I am one, I am two.* I talked to myself that way, like I was two people, one crazy, one almost ok. I said *There are people in this world who want to kill you. She is one of them.* And I let it sit in the open air for a bit, and the almost ok kid said *Go back inside go back to her she won't hurt you she's not mean you'll be safe there.* The voices in my head like wires crossing, I could believe either one, I could let them talk me into anything, one or the other. It didn't matter what became of me, I was with my voices and the shadow act of following my mother through the back lit streets.

Storms came, heavy ones that summer, the skies blackening, followed by the dark heavy rains over the city, the air stabbed again and again by lightning. The air was just as thick and heavy afterward. It didn't matter, nothing cooled the days down and at night the skies would be low and dark, filled it seemed with slow moving hot circling air that climbed inside your skin and made you long for water, a pool, anything cool. In those months of 1971, I effectively became a runaway, in some respects no different from lots of other kids living on the streets of Washington, D.C., forced out of bad home situations or without parents or guardians, soon to be caught up in the system put in place for homeless youth during these years. My mother had scheduled a date for a hearing before a judge to determine if I could be sent to Junior Village, a youth detention facility in the city's Shaw neighborhood. She'd first threatened it and finally made the phone call while I stood next to her. "I can't do this, I can't do this," she said over and over again, pushing her cigarette butts into the glass ashtray as she took another swig of scotch from the bottle she kept hidden behind the drapes in the living room. All I knew about Junior Village was what my mother told me: it was a place for troubled kids like me who had behavior problems and couldn't be controlled anymore. I might not survive a week there, she said, but that wasn't her problem anymore.

I didn't say anything, I didn't want to know what it meant, where she was sending me. It was no different to me than the foster home I'd been placed in some years before. Standing next to my mother in the half-light of late afternoon I wondered as I would often do in those years why she and Richard had adopted me in the first place, when it seemed as if they didn't really want a child. "Don't be ridiculous," she would say to me evenings when it was just the two of us, and she hadn't drunk much yet. "Of course we wanted you, he was always waiting for a son..." Her voice would trail off as it did, incomplete thought, then she'd look over toward me and say, "But that wasn't this," and her hand would make a motion in my direction, both dismissive and cognizant of my presence at the same time. We had come into these last days with one another with this odd understanding developing, as if in tacit agreement over the break that was replaying itself day after day, night after night. Her anger mixed with remorse. "My ghost child," she once called me. "My poor ghost child." The words laboring to make sense of the kid in front of her, the one on his way out into the night.

If I returned at all, it wasn't for more than a night or so, and I'd be sure to leave by early morning, before my mother woke, packing a bag of extra clothes, books, my glasses so I could read no matter where I was. I tried not to think about where I was going, what I would do day-to-day. I got up in people's yards, I woke from half sleep, cold and mosquito-bitten, found refuge in air-conditioned stores or apartment house lobbies during the day, hid at night in people's back yards. Sometimes the people who lived there would come out and I'd hide under their porch, as their footsteps would travel away from me and I'd come back out and lay on the cool plastic lawn chair, the plastic webbing imprinting itself on my legs and arms.

Some nights I spent in the basement with my Bolivian friend, José, but had to be out the next morning before the rest of the family woke. I'd be back out on the streets by 7 or 8, the air already heavy with humidity. Sometimes José and I would meet up later in the day, kick a soccer ball in the alley in back of my house. Sometimes Iris would come out into the back yard, stand at the gate and call for me to come back.

"You gotta go?" José would say, and I'd shrug, and say, "Nah, she'll go back inside soon enough," and we'd resume our game, sometimes joined by other kids from the neighborhood. As the light started to fade when it came time for everyone else to go in, I'd stand in between the entryways to both alleys, just stand and look down the asphalt leading to Porter Street and there would be the gear-grinding sound of the buses on Connecticut Avenue and the light would have started to deepen, so that I knew soon I'd have to be thinking about where to spend the night.

During the days the air was heavy and warm. Finding someplace to go wasn't ever that difficult, sometimes to José's house if no one else was home, mostly just walked around the neighborhood, from one end of that part of the city to the next. Went up to Wisconsin, down Wisconsin to Georgetown, sat on benches along the towpath, waited for someone to give me a dollar or two for lunch, headed back up Wisconsin with a sandwich and drink from one of the places up by Woodley, then made my way back up to Ordway. Over and over again. I went to the same places each day. I went to them again and again, as if already attempting to remember where I'd been just the day before, just an hour ago. I went up to the playground on Macomb Street I'd been going to since I was seven, played ping pong in the club house, the white ball struck against the back wall of the interior...Carom pool alone at the table for hours while the sun blazed outside. Through the doorway, I could see the neighborhood kids passing through the light and it was as if I'd become invisible to them, to anyone, no one noticed me or asked me what I was doing there, where I belonged or to which family. Sometimes, I stood in the flush damp heat and held the coins I'd brought for soda in my pocket and pressed the edges into my leg and waited for the familiar voices to emerge. *You can't be serious don't be so fucking dumb just take the stuff take it no one will care.* If the club house manager came he'd sometimes ask me to leave and I'd walk back down toward Connecticut Avenue, moving slowly down Newark Street and the hill that led back to the avenue. I'd go into People's Drug and Trover Book Shop, Safeway sometimes for food, and put things into my pockets or hide them under my t-shirt when no one was looking and head back up Ordway Street. As the light started to soften again, I would come down the alley back of our house and see the roofs in a row, like a line of stones above grass, and hear the morning doves in the trees and the bluing of dusk would enfold my body until it felt like the beginning of day all over again.

THIRTY-NINE

The days passed as they always had, blending into one another until they were all the same day, all the same night. I had no one to control me, no one to shelter or harm me. At night sitting with my books under a street light or in the doorway of an apartment building, I'd find my way back to another place, more still, certain, as in the torn paperback copy of *Walden* I kept with me through those days I'd found a way back in. "When my floor was dirty, I rose early, and, setting all my furniture out of doors on the grass, bed and bedstead making but one budget, dashed water on the floor, and sprinkled white sand from the pond on it, and then with a broom scrubbed it clean and white; and by the time the villagers had broken their fast the morning sun had dried my house sufficiently to allow me to move in again, and meditations were almost uninterrupted." The language of Thoreau became talismanic to me, so that I could open the pages anywhere in the course of my days and begin reading and lose my sense of time, place, the world to which I'd been brought.

One night, I found my way into the house of a neighbor two doors down. He'd returned late from one of the bars on Connecticut Avenue. I'd seen him coming up our street, staggering, weaving his way back up, and I'd kept behind a row of bushes and followed him as he moved, just as I'd followed my mother, watching him stop, unmoving, then walk just a bit behind and to the side, unable to take my eyes off him. His wife and children had gone away. I hadn't seen them most of the summer. She'd been a kind of neighborhood presence, inviting local children over to their house in the afternoons to have sandwiches and soda after school. Sometimes she'd let us play board games before we all headed back to our homes. That seemed like a long time ago, and then they'd disappeared and he'd be seen walking around the block at night, kind of a ritual, nothing special, nothing out of the ordinary, just his figure, there, kind of present, no one I knew or really could come close to. A father to kids I hardly knew either. Now there was no trace of them, and the man moving up the street in the darkness seemed disembodied, without direction or purpose as he climbed the hill.

I kept close behind him and when he went up the stairs of his back porch I stayed near, watching as he disappeared into an oblong frame of shadows. I stood for a time by the door, waiting, then saw the light go on upstairs, a face nearly visible at the window, its bony reflection apparent for a moment, then gone. The garden was wet, the grass unmowed and tall so that I could run my palms across the weighted spears with ease. I lay down, disappearing in a well of leaves and grass, and listened to the crickets and stared up at the window where the darkness filled the frame in soft reflective blots of blue and green. *What do you want here?* I asked myself. *What do you want with this poor guy who never did anything to you? What do you want to do with him? Why do you need to take from him?* I walked up the steps and moved as he had up the wooden planks and stood on the porch and pulled the door open. He'd left it unlocked and when I entered the kitchen I smelled the sour odors of meat that had gone bad, rotting fruit left out on the table in a bowl. He'd left the single hall light on and I saw the toys stacked up against one wall and some photographs of his kids on the table by the hallway and then there were the curtains, all of them ripped down from their rods and thrown onto the floor. The curtains were made of a heavy velvet fabric and I let them run through my hands like lengths of heavy rope, then let them fall back on the floor where I'd found them.

If he were awake....but the house was quiet as I moved through it in the ways I'd learned in my own house. I stood on the landing and looked into the room where he'd fallen asleep, half on, half off the bed. His shoes still on. His shirt slightly open at the chest so that I could see the shininess of his damp skin. I knelt by his bed and felt inside his trouser pocket. It was empty and I pulled my hand back out and listened to him breathing for awhile, his face a soft pale hue on the pillow as he breathed irregularly. The wallet was on the floor near his arm that had perhaps meant to reach for it, then let it go along with his keys. I opened it and took what money there was, not much, maybe $20, and left the wallet on the floor beside him, exactly as I'd found it.

The next afternoon I came by on my way down to the avenue and saw him in the garden, working his push mower across the small bit of lawn out back, a drink of tan liquid in his hand, as if he'd never gone away, never known any other day but this one. The sunlight formed a bruise over his left eye, and the bloodstains were still visible above his bandaged knee where he'd fallen the night before.

FORTY

While Richard was in Poland, my mother wrote him sometimes two or three times a day, informing him of daily life at home. As things worsened between us, my mother's letters to my father became more anguished and, at the same time, resigned to a state of affairs she felt she had no energy to control. Twenty-four years later, in the midst of packing up my apartment in Philadelphia, I would find several of these letters, still sealed in their envelopes, addressed to my father, c/o the American Embassy in Warsaw. He had apparently never opened them, never read my mother's words. What would they have meant at the time had he done so? What might he have felt for this woman so plainly unable to keep her life together any longer and in need of something, anything, from this man she had once adored, given her life to? Or are these even the right questions?

The letters remain the only other record I possess, besides the loose sheets of notepad, of my mother's life during these last months.

>Tuesday [postmarked June 9, 1971]
>Darling:
>I phoned up TWA this morning & they said your flight came in OK at Frankfurt and that it left on time yesterday. My goodness, you were a long while in getting to the airport. From 6 to 6:30 I was phoning up TWA at Dulles to find out whether you had checked in & would have told them to delay the flight you reached there, but the lines were busy all the while and we were frightened

also about tying up our own telephone so you wouldn't reach us. Anyway, it was a relief to hear your voice, and my goodness, was I glad you'd had a good meal before you left.

I know things have been very hard with us. But today I am missing you more than I can possibly tell you. (I ought to be able to get used to this, but I never have and never will.) I keep telling myself that 6 weeks will pass in a flash, and so it will. The main thing is for you to enjoy yourself after your assignment, but I hope and I am sure you will miss me too.

Coming back yesterday wasn't too bad, though it was bad enough with the congested traffic and the terrible thunderstorms. Over the bridge, a bus on the other side, splashed an ocean of water on to me, and I couldn't see for a minute. Actually, coming back took less than half an hour.

Nothing in the mail today; Andrew has half a day off & right now he's writing a note to you. He had a big lunch, went up by bike to get ice cream. Later he's going for a short bike ride.

Kenton went up so it's now 18 ½ . The others are the same. I'm resolved never to look at the stocks already sold. What's the sense.

Princess won't sleep with anyone and she is so morose I know she's missing you. Sammy sleeps on your bed downstairs.

It's bloody hot today, sunny, and chances are more thunderstorms. Tomatoes are coming on nicely and the hydrangeas for sure will be out this weekend.

We've just been visited by three tiny little girls who want to play with Princess, so Andy has taken them to the back garden & will give them some ice cream.

There's really nothing to tell you, but even this is nice

to know. Andrew has promised to be good, so let us cross our fingers and touch wood.

Every last ounce of my feelings go into BENEBUNES.

Your Iris Zowie

*

Saturday June 12 [postmarked June 12]

I hate to tell you this but Andrew has done the following:

Monday: stayed with José, whose family doesn't seem to know or care that he's there with them.

Tuesday: Came home early, had lunch and when I asked him where he had spent the night he said he didn't know. He left on his bicycle and didn't return home. I told him I forgave him for leaving the house and asked him to write Daddy.

Wednesday: I went with the police to check him in his paper route but we didn't find him.

Thursday: I phoned the school and discovered he was playing hooky, so I went to the swimming club and then all over Highland Place; the police couldn't help me so they told me to do what the School had also told me: get an appointment with Juvenile Court. I have the earliest appointment July 9th. During the night whilst I was asleep, and I had left both doors open for him, he came in with José and took all his clothes.

This was two or three hours after I had discovered them at the Uptown Cinema about 10 p.m. watching the movies. He refused to leave José.

He has stolen something like $25.00 from me.

Friday: Yesterday the Police came again because he, José and another boy had been caught stealing at Murphy's. They asked me whether I wanted him home but when they came they told me that the next time he was caught he would be put in a Receiving Home until he was 18. The two policemen said he needed a whipping.

Saturday: I asked him what he had done with the money he had stolen. He is now upstairs in his room and is kicking things. I am leaving him alone. I told him he can take his bike if he wants to; there is nothing I can do.

Benebunes
Iris

Friday was the first night he spent at home.

*

Monday [postmarked June 15]
Dear Richard:

As you can imagine, I have had the most grief-stricken week imaginable. I can only hope that Andrew is now truly sincere when he says he is very sorry and will never again do all the bad things he has been doing. I have told him to promise me two things: one, never to see José again to play with and two, just to obey me.

The whole trouble is that he is in love with José, just like he was with Miranda, and he doesn't have any other boys to play with. He doesn't want girlfriends & it seems that boys of his age just don't take to him. He has explained that he has an inferiority complex and this is why he wants to play with younger children.

Anyway, it seems that he will be getting a *Washington Star* paper route and this might have improving effect on him.

Probably we've both been hit hard by your not being here because we both miss you terribly. Even through all we've been through you are my husband and I cannot think of life without you. Andrew also no doubt felt that he could do just as he liked with your not being here. Anyway, he's really been on a big stealing binge...there must be about 20 paperback books he stolen either from the public library, or from 7 & Eleven. He's written in his name on all the fly leaves so I can't take them back. He's also been stealing money from me, but he denies taking the $25.00 on Saturday. He must have because it didn't mysteriously disappear and he rushed out of the house at 2 p.m. on Saturday, obviously to see José which he also denied but he came back home via the hydrangea bushes so I'm assuming he gave José the money.

For all our sakes, I'm just having to be patient with him. I even thought of calling up your friend and agreeing to his spending a week at the sea, but here gain, he'll get the feeling of irresponsibility and complete abandon and I won't know how to control him when he returns.

Richard, I had put off telling you these things because I didn't want to spoil your visit to Poland, but in the end I had to write to you about his activities, so that Andy would know he wasn't getting away with it all.

I've been feeling lousy, as you can imagine, but maybe things will really improve.

Incidentally, your check came for $440. And the rug is coming this week. I've cleaned the other two rugs with Safeway carpet cleaner.

In all my wanderings and constant searching for Andy I came across two nice Indian students at the corner house (they were the ones who told me they had seen Andy going to the movies with José). I thought it might be good for Andy, so I invited them for dinner on Wednesday night. They are nice, intelligent boys in their 20's.

Are you having a wonderful time in Poland? I imagine

you must feel terribly sad at times.

I can't tell you how much I miss our old life. For me, this is going to be the longest 6 weeks.

I love you,

          Benebunes,

                Iris

P.S. When your bad boy comes home from school today I am going to make him write you a long letter which maybe will cleanse his soul.

*

Monday
June 21 [postmarked 22 June]

Darling:

Aside from 2 postcards & one short letter I haven't received anything else from you but you did warn me not to expect too much!

I imagine you are having a very interesting time and are seeing lots of people.

Here everything is the same — Andrew's behavior has been extremely bad but there's no sense in worrying you about this.

Last week I phoned up that nice Mrs. K. and we were all set that I would drive Andrew to her place at 7 a.m. this morning for they were all going to the bus depot to journey to Ocean City. Andrew hadn't wanted to go, saying he doesn't like her daughters, so late last night I phoned Mrs. K. that it was "off." He just doesn't want to leave home. She understood and told me she had been "through the rivers" with some of hers and we promised that we would have a real get-together when she returns. I will look forward to meeting her very much.

I cannot get Andrew away from José. He has the same mad obsession with this boy as he had for the girl down the block from us, Miranda (I told you about her before, but maybe you've forgotten). This is why he wants to stay home to be near the boy. He comes home about 11 p.m. and last night I had to prowl the neighborhood to get him. I found him back of their garden & hidden there were 2 repeat 2 Safeway carts.

They go on stealing rampages and the next time Andrew is caught & the Police arrest him I am going to tell them to keep him!

Here the weather has turned terribly hot & thank goodness for the air conditioner.

Only once have I seen a 6000 BTU A/C for less than $150 and that is a Fedders for $135.00. I wonder if I should buy it?

I don't need to tell you that I miss you – it seems the time will never pas until your return.

Benebunes,
Iris

*

These letters tell one part of the story. A woman feeling the burden of each day with a son she could no longer understand or care for and a husband she believed had abandoned her. And yet….There is another portion of the record that Iris kept, contained in the notes she wrote in the pages of the drugstore tablet that used to sit next to the telephone in our house, then became a fixture on the glass table in front of the sofa where she sat, most often alone, with her glass of gin or Scotch, a cigarette in hand, the pad resting near the ashtray. Every so often she'd take it up again, re-read the prior day's notes, add new information, an accounting that years later I'm uncertain how to judge. Who was my mother writing for? What did she hope to do with this collection of "evidence" that seemed intent on documenting every illicit, awful thing I'd done that summer? Was Richard her audience? Me? Someone else she imagined would come upon these notes years later and understand their meaning? Or simply her own wayward self, locked into this deadly game of cat and mouse with her runaway, adopted son? I don't know. I'll never know. I have the pages, preserved in plastic, reminders of how my mother lived and what she thought those days of her last summer.

> The $25.00 he previously stole from me must have been given to Athena or placed in hiding there — this after he promised to be a good boy.
>
> He refuses to leave Athena alone & presumably they still are stealing together.
>
> The last time I went to that house I discovered Andrew with Athena in their basement at 11.30p. Knocked on back door & about 4 men & women came out — shouted Andrew was not there — meanwhile he had left by the basement door as I saw him.

WED 7 TOOK STEAK BAG AT 2 PM
LAST I SAW OF HIM.
WANTED TO KNOW WHERE
HE GOT BOOK I FOUND
IN PEG BIN.
LATER CONFESSED IT
CAME FROM TROVERS
(I HAD TAKEN IT FROM
HIM. 5 MINS LATER IT
DISAPPEARED. HE SAID
HE'D NEVER SEEN THIS
BOOK.) FOUND IT UNDER
STOVE. CALLED UP TROVERS
& MADE HIM RETURN BOOK)

THU 8 CAME BACK LATE AT NIGHT
WEARING NEW SWEATER.
REFUSED TO SPEAK TO ME

FRI 9 CONFESSED STOLE SWEATER
AT WOODY'S. WENT TO
CHEVY CHASE CLUB
HELPED HIMSELF TO GINGER
ALE + PEANUTS IN
BALLROOM. HAD ICE
CREAM ON TERRACES + TOLD
THEM TO CHARGE IT.
SAID THAT WEEK HE'D
TAKEN CHOCOLATE BARS AT
VARIOUS STORES

       HAD A LONG LOVING TALK
WITH HIM NOT TO STEAL
OR LIE ANY MORE

SAT 10 FOUND NEW PAPER
BACK NOVEL IN WOOD
LOGS. WAS FURIOUS.
HE SPITS AT ME —
LAUGHS AT ME +
SAYS FUCK YOU —
I TELL HIM GET OUT

SUN 11 STILL OUT. DISCOVER
NEARLY $1.00 IN ~~ANY~~
THE TICKET BOX —
ALL THE 9 BOOKS OF
BUS TICKETS GONE

One day when we went over to S's to K around 7 pm, I told him he could play all day provided he was back at 6 pm. He came back @ 9 pm all ready. I told him to take a shower & he said he wanted to watch TV. Said he couldn't so he rushed outside to get on his bike. I padlocked it just in time & returned to phone K. Then I saw him remove the padlock so I went & punctured the tire. This is the ninth he called me an old bitch & kicked me — he has also thrown my pillow at me

---

— the silver bowl

JULY 11 SUN

Trespassers 2942 Sydney

Khadduri:
            244-4454

Both boys Kheoparanee, steal-ing throughout house — stealing money + food from parents

American University

Officer Clark
8th Precinct

Iris kept to her own counsel these waning days of summer, the tablet a kind of testimony, potentially comforting, as she sought to understand the events as they were happening to her. A son gone missing….His thefts…A record of his having run off again. And when she looked up from her writing, the pad pushed aside, her pencil resting atop the pages of re-constructed narrative, of acts committed, violations held before her again? "This is the night he called me an old bitch." No effort to conceal what was in plain sight, the words forming a provisional daybook not meant for anyone else's eyes. "He also threw my pills at me." Years later the sound of her hands moving the pages back into place, replacing them in the drawer where she kept them, her eyes not traveling far to see that in a few hours it would be night again.

How much peace, she may have thought, how much comfort can any one of us provide another. And, the pencil pushed aside a final time, how little remains to be said after all.

FORTY-ONE

Six months and four days after the last letter I have of my mother to my father from that summer of 1971, Iris died on Christmas Eve. I had not seen her since the end of the summer, when I was taken to a Catholic boarding school in Spring Grove, Pennsylvania, about three hours from Washington. Over the years, multiple, often contradictory versions of what happened that night have emerged. In the story I was first told by my father, he'd returned to our house on Ordway Street to pick up some clothes, papers, things he needed. He and my mother had been separated for several weeks following his return from Poland. I don't know where he was living, perhaps with friends, perhaps he took a room as he did off and on throughout the years of their marriage. As my father related events to me, he came into the house and saw Iris on the sofa in the front room, the *New York Times* crossword puzzle on her lap, a pencil in her hand. She was not moving. When he came closer he realized that she was already dead. He called the ambulance, and when the medics came they confirmed that there was nothing to be done. She had been dead for at least several hours.

I would hear this story for the first time the next day, Christmas morning, when my father arrived at the apartment of a friend of his, Joanna, who had offered to have me stay with her through the Christmas break from school.

"Andy," my father had said to me in Joanna's living room early in the day on Christmas Eve, "there's no point in you coming down to my office and sitting there with nothing to do until 2 in the morning. You should have a nice time, be with people, have some fun."

"Your daddy's right," Joanna said. "We can have Vigilia with Barbara and her girls. What do you say, Andy? Sound like something good?"

I'd spoken with my mother the previous morning, when she'd asked me to come by to help with the gutters. Somehow she'd found where I'd been staying and gotten the phone number from one of Richard's friends at Voice. "Let me check with daddy first," I'd said, in what was our last phone conversation. "You do that, pet, that's fine, and hopefully I'll see you soon." She sounded like she'd already been drinking and when I called my father, he said, "Andy, absolutely not, you must not go there, let me speak to Iris myself."

I looked up at Joanna and said, "Yeah, sure, that'd be nice," and walked back into the guest room and sat on the bed and heard my father speaking in Polish.

"Jesteś bardzo słodki, aby dbać o Andrew," my father said.

"Nie martw się, będzie z nami dobry."

"Merry Christmas, Joanna."

"Merry Christmas, Richard." After that, he was gone.

At dinner that night we had the typical fish dishes served in Polish households on Christmas Eve and opened presents together under the large tree in their living room. A little after 11 we all drove together to a nearby Catholic church for midnight mass. We returned to Joanna's apartment around 1:30. The next morning shortly after my father arrived, I heard him in the entryway to Joanna's apartment speaking to her. A few minutes later he appeared at the doorway to the bedroom. He was wearing a new jacket and trousers. When I asked him how he'd changed his clothes since the day before (as far as I knew he hadn't returned to our house on Ordway Street), he said that he'd picked up a few things from home. He sat down with me on the bed and took my hands into his. His voice was soft. I recall his hands taking mine into his before the words formed in his mouth, "Andy... your mother is dead....Iris...she is dead....."

   I turned away from him and began to cry, not knowing why exactly, not even sure what it meant that my mother was gone. Joanna wandered in for a moment, then turned and left without speaking. Later, I would go to her, and she would say to me, "Andy, you know you come here if you need, if your father needs something, he can come here with you, you are both welcome here...." I took a soft pillow from her sofa and placed it over my knees and glanced up at her and saw she had been crying. When we left, she gave me ten dollars and said I should buy something little for myself, something to wear for later.

   In the late afternoon, my father took me back to our house. We walked into rooms I had not seen since August. The sofa on which my mother had died held the light acrid odors of urine and throw up. When I knelt down and looked underneath I found a short pencil in need of sharpening. I went through each room in the house looking for evidence of what had happened. The mattress in her bedroom had been stripped of sheets and covers. By her? In the dresser drawer I found empty bottles of pills, sleeping aids prescribed by our family doctor. My father said nothing at the time, nothing to suggest that Iris had taken her own life. I was either too young to question him further or not able to face what might have seemed obvious at the time.

   How had my mother died? When the report came back from the coroner, my father told me Iris had died of a massive heart attack brought on by a blood clot on her right lung. My mother, who had smoked up to three packs a day of Marlboros to the end of her life, had rejected her doctor's advice that she quit smoking and at least reduce the amount of alcohol she drank each day. In this way, the report from the coroner, which I never saw, made sense. My mother had died of a massive heart attack. What more needed to be said? For years it was the only story I needed or could tell: blood clot on her lung, went to her heart. She died instantly.

FORTY-TWO

The last time I'd seen my mother alive, I'd come home for Thanksgiving break. The weather in Washington had been unseasonably warm that fall, though by November had shifted into the low 50's and upper 40's. The trees were bare on the avenue and on our street the maples and elms had the uprooted look of trees I'd seen in etchings by Goya at the National Gallery.

Iris, my father explained to me on the ride from the train station, had just returned from the hospital, following another stay for what my father referred to as "bad nerves." I didn't ask what this meant, having long heard my father use this description for other periods when my mother would disappear for days on end for bed rest.

From the street I could see the windows of the second floor were still open to the night air when we arrived. For some reason the screens had been removed from the windows and lay in a pile in the front yard. One light shone from inside the bedroom in the front of the house, while downstairs I could see that all the lights were on. Depositing me with my few bags, my father prepared to go back to work for his night shift at Voice of America. I took my bags upstairs to my bedroom and sat on the bed in the dark while outside the wind was starting up and I could feel the cold air coming in through the partly opened window. Downstairs I could hear them talking as Richard gathered up his work materials and my mother seemed to be following him from room to room.

"You could have kept him away longer," I heard her say,

then: "What do you want me to do with him if he doesn't behave?" He didn't respond but I could hear him coming up the stairs and when he came down the hall, he stood in the doorway to my room and blew me a kiss and told me to obey Iris and that he would be back tomorrow to check on me. He turned and walked back down the stairs and moved past Iris who apparently was waiting for him at the bottom of the staircase, then closed the door behind him and went out into the Washington evening.

Sometime before I returned for Thanksgiving break, my father had moved out of our house again, this for the last time, to an apartment on Connecticut just down from the zoo. I didn't know where he was, only that it was a nice small one-room studio and that his windows overlooked Rock Creek Park. His absence from Ordway Street wasn't surprising or unusual, just ordinary movement between "homes", otherwise nothing new. After my father had left, I walked down the hall and opened the door to his bedroom and saw that the room was bare of any personal belongings except for his bed and the desk at which he used to sit and prepare for work. The closet was empty, though still had the smell of mothballs from the summer when woolens had been stored here.

I hadn't slept in my room in over two months, and I noticed that the shelves had been cleared of my books and metal cars and plastic model boxes, and the remainder of my clothes had been removed from the closet, the shelves bare and dark in the shadowy light. I didn't know why I was here, this room that was no longer my room, and as I sat down on the bed I thought of where I could go. José was gone, had been taken back to Cochabamba by his mother, who at the end of our summer saw that America was not doing her son any good and took him back to his country.

I sat on the bed and leaned into the draughts of air from the open window and smelled wood smoke from across the way and could see up the alley where we'd played soccer all summer, now quiet and deserted. There seemed nothing in the world as quiet and isolated as this place, and I took out of my knapsack my reading glasses, and a book of stories by Chekhov that my mother had kept in her room and that I'd taken one night a long time ago but she'd never noticed as missing, or at least hadn't said so.

An hour or so later, I heard my mother call for me. "Andrew! Andrew! Come down, help me make some soup."

I stood by the empty space near my bed and looked over the pile of boxes that had been gathered there and gazed out the window toward our neighbors across the alley, and my mother called up to me again, "Andrew, please come help me, I need to eat something." Her voice was like this strange echo of a voice I'd heard often before, but this time was different. I sat on the bed and didn't move and she kept calling up to me and I kept not moving, willed myself not to move. I said to myself *you can't you can't you just stay here don't go down* so that it was maybe a quarter hour or so of my not moving and her calling, then silence and the sound of the phone being dialed as she called my father.

"No, Richieu," I heard her say, "he's not doing what I ask, he's not helping me, he refuses to come down. For Christ's sake he won't even help me make some soup. No...No, Richieu, you come get him, come get him and take him with you, I don't want him here."

When I finally came down, my mother was off the phone. Her ashtray was piled high with ash and half-smoked cigarettes and she had started a second bottle of gin, having finished the first one and left it out on the table. All of it was too familiar, and I started to turn to go back upstairs and wait for my father. But she motioned for me to stay, to listen.

"I am through," Iris said, "I can't do this anymore. You know, I've tried so hard, we both have, your father and I. But you've taken all my love, and now there's none left to give." The words made their own individual sounds in the air and I wondered what to make of them. Another finality? Another sending off?

"I won't see you ever again, Andrew. As far as I'm concerned, you've broken anything I have left to offer. I have no love left, you've taken it all."

There was a rhythm to these endings, a way I saw them as part of one long conversation that had never stopped, never would stop. Her voice re-circled, came back into itself, having volition but no destination, no new place it could go.

And I stood as I'd stood nights and days and afternoons and parts of evenings for as long as I could remember.

"What do you want to tell me?" my mother said.

I kept my hands close to my sides and saw that it was already late morning and my father would be coming soon to take me away.

"Nothing."

"Don't you have anything to say?" she asked me. "No response?"

It was like a cataract had formed in my eye, and I couldn't focus. I tried to imagine that my vision was coming through another, as if I weren't one but two, and she was an object in the distance, so I had to steady my vision and focus hard as the lines blurred and she became indistinct, unrecognizable.

I stood silently, while my mother went back to her drink.

When my father came home, he asked me what had happened, and I said I didn't know. My mother was standing in the corridor and I was telling him I didn't know and on the table in the dining room were her papers and typewriter and a bowl of soup.

She looked over at us and said, "You might as well take it out of here just take it with you," and I knew she was referring to me, but it didn't matter. She picked up her spoon and started eating the soup. It was almost 1:30 in the afternoon by then, a Tuesday. In two days it would be Thanksgiving.

My father collected my things and brought them downstairs and put them by the door and asked my mother if she needed anything. She gestured with her hands, waving us off. He picked up the suitcase and we went out into the cool afternoon, the light hard and sharp on us as we closed the door and walked down the steps toward the avenue.

FORTY-THREE

The morning of Friday, December 24, 1971 broke cloudy and cool, in the low 40's according to *The Washington Post*. The front page from that day included stories bearing the following headlines: "Mujibur, Bhutto To Meet," "India to Start Repatriation Of Refugees Within Week," "Hoffa Gets Out Of Jail," and "Food Stamp Suit Demands 'Nutritionally Adequate Diet." Inside the front section of the paper, ads for Christmas Eve services in the city filled two adjoining pages, among them All Souls Episcopal, the church we attended, listing Reverend Frank Blackwelder, D.D., Rector, with a Christmas Eve service to be held at 8:00 p.m. The following day, Christmas Day, Holy Communion would be offered at 11:00 a.m. Advertisements in the entertainment section featured Henry Fonda, Jane Alexander, and Richard Dreyfus in Aram Saroyan's *The Time of Your Life* at the Kennedy Center's Eisenhower Theatre. The film, *Harold and Maude,* with Bud Court and Ruth Gordon, had opened at the Avalon and Mike Nichols' *Carnal Knowledge* was playing at the Cinema 7 at Seven Corners in that Virginia suburb. A story in the Metro Section focused on impoverished families in southwest Washington unable to afford Christmas lights and dependent on a local church for food donations.

The day would have begun as it always did. Iris rose early that day and went downstairs in the crisp December air to feed "the animals," as Richard referred to the beagle and tabby cat that had been family pets for many years, before she unlocked and opened the front door, going down the six cement steps and retrieving the paper from the middle of the front walkway where it always was. Sometimes it was thrown onto the lawn, and Iris would go out barefoot to retrieve it, but this morning she wore her slippers and grabbed the paper from the walk and returned to the porch. She noticed the Coldwell Banker Realty sign askew on the front lawn, listing the house for sale. The sign, removed and replaced several times over the last many months, was barely visible across the tops of the bushes that fronted the house, yet in the morning light the black frame hung just slightly in view, as if through some trick of sight it could simultaneously appear and disappear. The lawn showed the ragged, yellow patches of grass in need of re-sodding, something that had been planned numerous times over the summer, then put off as each time my mother calculated the cost and decided there wasn't enough money to cover it.

Standing on the front porch, in the time it took to notice that the neighbors' house immediately to the left was empty, Iris saw lights on in the Leonard house across the street and in other houses down the hill and considered again, as she had often done with me before we set out on our walks, the length of time it took to walk from the corner of Connecticut Avenue to the place where she was standing: a full seven minutes from the corner of Connecticut and Ordway to her front porch. She estimated the time it would take today for her, with her right foot still bothering her from a fall the week before, to make it down the hill to the Safeway for food for the next several days over the holiday and to Woodley Liquors next door.

She looked around and saw the house needed straightening. No one to help with that, she realized, and wondered aloud about the time it would take to dust and vacuum the house. Then the time remaining before she would need to ask him again for a check. She had checked her account at Riggs last week...or the week before that.... There had been $74.00 in the account or was it $47.00? She couldn't remember, the numbers moving in columns of blue and green ink, as once she'd written down the monthly balance on a yellow legal pad she kept in the escritoire drawer. She did the sums in her head, standing at the entrance now and peering back out into the morning light. The numbers crossed in Iris's mind, crossed and re-crossed, until she gave up counting. She went back inside, closed the door and sat down on the sofa and heard the dog and cat in the kitchen waiting to be let out. She sat there for several minutes more before getting up and walking through the swinging door in the dining room into the kitchen and opening the back door and watching as they raced out into the cold morning air, one after the other, the cast first, then the dog, both disappearing into the garden and the shadows of the morning light that fell across the sloping lawn.

Iris opened the fridge and took out the milk, set it on the counter, noted it was almost gone, entered "milk" on her mental shopping list, boiled water for coffee, waited the several minutes it took for the whistle to go off, looked up at the clock and saw it was 8:17 a.m., poured the water over the crystals of Taster's Choice she'd scooped out of the red-lidded jar, added some milk, spooned out a half teaspoon of sugar from the sugar bowl on the aluminum table next to the stove, stirred lightly, and moved with her coffee back into the front room.

The wind-up clock on the mantle showed the time as

12:32, though it had showed that time for days, perhaps weeks now. Iris couldn't remember when the clock had stopped, which day it was, but somehow this morning she felt no urge to wind it from the back and set the gears going again. She drank her coffee and looked at the paper on the table, turning it over so that she could read the headlines below the fold. "FCC Decides to Drop Probe of Bell System." "CIA Force Imperiled by Reds in Laos." "Bhutto's Old Views Submerged in Crisis." Iris had mostly stopped following the events in Pakistan, having turned away from its history and politics some years back, even as India and Pakistan had once been primary bases of knowledge during her working years as a journalist. The Indo-Pakistani war that had unfolded over the last several months recalled for her some necessary but nearly forgotten piece of her own history, as if she had stepped away from herself and left items of her British upbringing back in some distant dislocated place. Richard was at her side, she remembered, when the latest conflict between India and Pakistan had broken out. That was in mid-December. He had come by in the late afternoon to get some things. She couldn't remember what. He had sat with her, and they had a drink together. They'd spoken about me and my schooling and what would happen to the house should the trial separation become permanent and divorce finalized as a result. The day's paper had been left behind, she had almost forgotten to glance at it, when he noticed it and said something about the war and how India would react and what East Pakistan was likely to do in response. She had stopped drinking from her glass half-filled with Scotch and looked up at the clock on the mantle and saw that it was 4:32. That was some days ago and she couldn't remember how they'd left things, whether he'd be returning before the new year, where the boy would be staying until he returned to school in Pennsylvania, how many days she had to respond to the legal documents he'd left for her to read and sign.

Iris got up when she heard the dog at the back door, whining to be let in, and went into the kitchen and opened the back door and pushed the screen door wide to let her back inside. The air was softer now, absorbed in sunlight that had come through the trees, momentarily lifting the grey. Iris believed that it was a sign of things to come, the light always told the story of the day she had said many times: the light falls in the morning laying down the patterns for the day, darkness and light, the patterns are fused sometimes, so you can barely negotiate them, but there is always that moment when one band of light crosses another and you can see the prospect of the day ahead. The back garden opened into a shaded pool and the light formed a bar of resin-like fluid covering one part of the garden, where the fence separated the property from the alley. Iris noted the play of light through the leaves, the abrupt distillation of color that seemed to emerge from the back of a dark space, as in Vermeer's "Young Woman with a Water Jug," the woman framed in that temperate space between the partly opened window and the table on which rested the silver jug, half caught in shadow, half suffused with light that seemed to emanate from nowhere but inside the room itself. Iris saw from the back porch landing that the garden was much in need of repair, that the fence separating the property from their neighbor's had been torn wide again, perhaps by dogs that had gotten in somehow. She remembered she had the name of the handyman somewhere inside, the phone next to the sofa in the dining room, on the table, she could see it in her mind's eye, with other numbers she'd written down over the months, for the electric company, Riggs Bank, Sibley Hospital emergency.

The notepad rested where she had left it and when she noticed it again she realized she hadn't written a word since August. There had been a series of notes she was preparing, then stopped, leaving them incomplete, eventually ripping them out of the tablet, crumpling them and throwing them in the trash. She had composed notes to remind herself of what needed to be done, then had abandoned these as well, jotting figures instead in the margins of the pages, sums to keep track of: how much was owed on the mortgage, electric, water, her end of month balance at Riggs Bank, etc. The figures broke into columns, the columns went down the page, were added up, subtracted, sometimes divided, new figures emerging from each column. At night she sometimes sat with these numbers a long while, pausing before each new mark, wondering how it was that these figures made any sense, what meaning they could have. Richard had usually taken care of the bills. Now it was up to her. There wasn't enough; he hadn't left her enough. She was aware of that. *Two homes*, he said to her, *two homes, Iris. It's very expensive for us to live this way.* The answer to that was obvious, but she saw no need to remind him of what he already knew.

The electric had gone past due, then been shut off, then turned back on. Same with the gas. Now it was on. Soon, she realized, it would be off again. The bills came, and she sorted through them and left them in a pile on the front table by the door for him to review when he came by. She couldn't say when he would come by. Sometimes, it was weeks. The bills were on the table, and sometimes he would come by when she was out and take them. Some of them were paid and some wouldn't have been. She looked at it as his having his way.

The morning nearing its ending, she prepared for her day. A brown wool skirt, pink cashmere jumper her sister sent her from Marks & Spencer several years ago, blue wool socks, black knee high boots she'd bought for herself on sale at Casual Corner, even though at $18.99, they were still more expensive than she felt she could afford. At a little after 12, the day having turned and the light grown sharper, she set out for the stores on Connecticut Avenue. The street was empty as she walked past the house where she and I had once stopped for wood and a woman had come out and asked if we needed any help and a girl behind her had appeared, her face masked in shadow before she disappeared entirely. When Iris reached the corner of Ordway and Connecticut, the Riggs Bank clock would have showed the time as 12:11 p.m. and the temperature as 44 degrees Fahrenheit. An elderly man across the street disembarked from an L4 bus and crossed Connecticut as the bus waited at the light. She recognized him as a neighbor who'd once lived a few doors down and had later settled in the apartment house on the corner after his wife had passed away. He walked slowly, one hand holding a bag of groceries and the other some giftwrap rolls tied with string. When their paths crossed midway in the street, she glanced quickly over at him and realized he didn't remember her and turned briefly when she'd reached the opposite corner to watch him walking slowly up the steps of the apartment house. A moment later, he disappeared.

When she came into the Safeway, she saw that the front of the store was decorated with Christmas ornaments and lights and fruitcakes. Other Christmas desserts were laid out on metal display shelves. She walked down the soup aisle and found the Campbell's display and picked out a can of cream of mushroom soup. She remembered that she needed milk and went to the dairy case and pulled out a quart of whole milk, then went down the bread aisle and picked out a loaf of rye bread with caraway seeds. Iris laid these items on the black belt of the checkout and watched the cashier punch in the numbers into the register, while she fished for spare change and dollar bills in her purse. The total came to $3.29. Iris took out three one dollar bills and two quarters and gave these to the cashier and without saying a word took her change and the bag containing the soup, milk and bread and headed out into the day again. Behind her the cashier had started to ring up the next customer. Iris wasn't able to remember if she had closed her purse and put the bag down on the ground and looked down and saw the purse was still open and snapped it closed and picked the bag of groceries up again. She next went into Woodley Liquor where she bought a fifth of Gilbey's gin and a 16 oz. bottle of Schweppes tonic water.

The light had changed as she reached the corner and, as she stood there with her bags in either hand, she noticed that the bank was advertising saving bonds for the new year. A ring of Christmas wreaths hung from the bank's columns inside, and the light shone yellow and white through the frosted windows coated in sprayed-on artificial snow.

The day went slowly into afternoon. There was the threat of snow in the air, as winter storm clouds persisted. Iris resisted the urge at first to pour herself a first drink, then did so anyway. She picked up the book she had been reading weeks earlier and noticed that it was one of her favorites from before the war, E.M. Forster's *A Passage to India*. She began reading at random from the book, failing to remember where she'd stopped, but not caring, anywhere she started up again was familiar and brought her back to a world that still remained familiar to her: "A ghost followed the ship up the Red Sea, but failed to enter the Mediterranean. Somewhere about Suez there is always a social change: the arrangements of Asia weaken and those of Europe begin to be felt." Iris read at this language, maybe a bit more, then laid the book aside on the table. She had read the passage many times, the same lines again and again. She knew them almost by heart, since the first time she'd encountered them as a young woman in the '30's in London, could recite them, as once she had spent an afternoon just like this one in late November, reading a narrative that over time came to resemble the shape of her own imagination as it returned to its unsettled roots.

She could remember so many things. Couldn't remember so many others. A woman from her childhood lifted a cloth to reveal the death mask of her mother. Another woman came near their carriage on a London morning as she was about to be taken to her father's house in the country. *The sea stretched like silk across the bay.* Brighton Beach.... She was taking up stones and rubbing her hands across their smooth grey surfaces. Stone after stone pressed against her palms, while behind her she could hear the voices of her mother and father and sisters.... *It was so calm, it was so quiet.* The sea moving past, her days moving past the sea. She dreamt it was a gull that came light and dark and landed near her and after that nothing but the sound of its cries in the thin January air of the seacoast just down the road from the house where.... No one lived there anymore. She heard the words in her head before she could imagine a reason for saying them. One was and wasn't here. One needed and didn't need to say anything.

She placed the drink down on the floor. Laid her own body down next to the drink on the floor. The light had stopped being astonishing to her. She understood what Richard had meant when he said to her, "You will live to see the day you don't want to live anymore." The morning was far away. The afternoon was not yet over.

"Flesh and bone," Iris said to herself. "Blood is thicker than water. There is a beginning and an after. After we met...after the last time you came here...after you swore you would return to me...after the light had parted...after your name was taken from us....after the great body of your life's work was finished...There is a beginning and after...." She stopped, stood and went up the stairs to her bedroom and removed a bottle of pills from the top drawer of her dresser. She placed the bottle on the bed next to her and opened the window to let the cool air in. She thought she heard pigeons cooing in the limbs of the elm tree outside. She thought she smelled smoke from a neighbor's fireplace. Air was lighter than smoke, smoke heavier than light.

The seco-barbitol took several minutes to act on her system. Fifteen minutes at most. She took the pills with a swig of gin, finishing off the bottle. Iris went into Richard's closet and pulled from the belt rack one of the belts he hadn't taken with him. A 42" waist, black full grain cowhide, silver buckle. She understood that the pills alone should suffice to cause heart failure, but wanted to be certain this time.

Iris went back into her bedroom where the closet was to the right of the doorway and secured the belt over the steel rod on which her clothes hung, making sure as she did so to tie the belt twice around the rod. Closing the door firmly so that she was in full darkness, she placed the looped end with the buckle around her neck and dropped slowly to her knees and let her body's weight do the rest.

Approximately fifteen seconds later, she lost consciousness. In another minute and a half, her body began to lose muscle tone. Four and a half minutes later, she ceased moving altogether. Death came shortly after that.

*

When my father came into the house that night, expecting to find Iris waiting for him, perhaps offering some kind of reconciliation on Christmas Eve, he noticed that the papers had been left on the glass table and the ashtrays were filled with ash from recently smoked cigarettes. The cat and dog were anxiously waiting for him by the door.

My father came into a darkened living room and looked for a moment into the darkness before switching on the ceiling light, punching the black button of the light switch on the wall next to the front door. He observed an empty room, except for the books and newspapers on the glass coffee table and my mother's opened bottle of gin and emptied glass. He called out to Iris, and walked through the dining room into the den and his bathroom where he showered in the mornings before work, finally arriving in the kitchen. Switching on the lights as he went through each room, he saw the evidence of her last day: the soup bowl and bread plate from her late lunch still on the table, the empty can of soup on the counter in the kitchen, the bread still in its plastic, an unopened carton of milk in the fridge. Little else in the way of food.

He turned to the hallway and left the kitchen and walked up the stairs and took a left at the top of the landing and went into my bedroom first and saw that the bed was stripped, only the bare mattress and my pillows resting at the head under the window. The closet door was closed, as he opened it and looked inside and saw that some of my clothes had remained, most taken with me when I'd left for boarding school in August. He left my room and walked back down the hall and looked into what had been his bedroom and glanced into his closet, calling out quietly just before opening the door and again just after. By the time he reached Iris's bedroom, he understood and paused at the doorway for a moment before entering and saw the bed unmade and the bottle of pills on the dresser, emptied. He whispered her name and stopped himself before opening the door of her closet. Her body was slumped in its final position, her knees slightly bent, her head dipped and at an angle, the black leather of the belt forming a blue-black bruise around her neck.

Richard untied the belt from the rod and held his wife's heavy body against his for a moment, letting it rest on the cool wood floor while he went to the telephone by her bedside and called for an ambulance.

After they had taken her body away, my father wept, wordlessly crying in the sharp December night as he sat on the front porch. After several minutes, he went back inside the house where the animals awaited him and fell asleep on the living room sofa where he would tell me the next day that my mother had died suddenly of a heart attack while doing *The New York Times* crossword puzzle.

Iris's last day, he would say to me, was perfectly normal.

Mrs. Iris Mossin, Former Journalist

Mrs. Richard Mossin, 51, a travel agent and former journalist, died Friday at her home, 2906 Ordway St. NW, after a short illness.

Mrs. Mossin, the former Iris Alford, was born in London and attended the London School of Economics. From 1943 to 1948 she worked as a London correspondent for United Press.

Mrs. Mossin came to this country in 1951 and worked for the London News Chronicle in New York. She came to Washington in 1951 as a correspondent for the International Foreign News Service.

Besides her husband, she leaves a son, Andrew R., and three sisters in London.

Services will be held at 8 p.m. Wednesday at Joseph Gawler's Sons Funeral Home, 5130 Wisconsin Ave. NW.

FORTY-FOUR

The day after the day after. I woke early to an empty house, my father having left for work already. I listened for the familiar song of the mourning doves, but there was only silence, the trees cold and still with a trace of light snowfall from the night before. The gutters were blue grey in the morning light, and a branch rested at an odd angle against the side of the house. The back alley was deserted, and up the hill I spotted the laundry freshly hung from the clothesline of the Robertson house and beyond that, on the other side of 30th, heard wood being sawed for fireplace logs. My clock radio showed the time to be 7:47 a.m. I left my bed in t-shirt and underpants, walking over cold wood into the bathroom. I came back out into the hall and noticed the night-light that'd gone out in the baseboard socket. I walked past my father's room and into my mother's. The door had been left open and the windows partly opened, so that the cold air from outside flowed into the room. My mother's bed had been stripped of sheets and blankets, though it wasn't clear to me when this happened or what had been done with the bed linens.

I opened my mother's dresser drawers one by one, from the top to the bottom drawer, five drawers in all. The top drawer had been mostly cleaned out, none of my mother's medication bottles remaining. Some bracelets, a ring, a few sets of earrings in a corner of the drawer. The next drawer down had a few sweaters, a cardigan my mother wore rarely, a pair of black trousers that I'd never seen her wear. The last three drawers contained odds and ends of clothing, as if everything had already been picked over, stockings and underwear and mismatched knee-high socks clumped in small piles in each drawer. And from each drawer the remnant odors of my mother's body, nearly sweet, partly acrid.

The closet was filled with her dresses and skirts, a few belts still hanging from one side of the bar, the dresses pushed over so that a partition remained between the belts and the dresses. A small scar marked the middle of the bar and I slid my finger across it to feel the raise in the metal. Turning to face the bed and night tables on either side, I noticed that my mother's ashtray and usual collection of pill containers and glasses had been removed. The table nearest the left side of the bed, the one my mother preferred for sleeping, had been recently wiped down, so that only a few traces of ash remained. On the surface of the wood laminate, the multiple dark imprints of cigarette burns appeared like small islands on a map, each corrugated edge floating atop the dark blonde wood that formed borders of light and dark.

The stairs leading down to the first floor were clean and free of the usual pile of shoes and other belongings kept to one side. I didn't recall if this was how the stairs looked the day before, if there had been things left out or if perhaps my father had already taken whatever remained and brought things back into the rooms where they belonged. I walked into the living room and over to the sofa and sat down where my mother had been sitting two nights before and traced with my finger a small line of ash from one of the mostly emptied ash trays and saw that the silver tray bore the stains from condensation where glasses of cold liquid had been placed, and I worked my finger through each circle so that it was like watching the movement of a splinter worked from underneath the skin and, as I did so, I recognized that the tray would have to be polished to remove the condensation marks. I wondered if we still had silver polish underneath the sink where my mother had kept it and occasionally had me bring it out to clean what little silver my mother possessed: two candelabra, a set of flatware she kept in a wooden cutlery box, the serving tray that had once rested on the dining room table.

The house was cold, I realized for the first time, and went to the thermostat and turned the heat up to 72 and listened to the sound of the furnace coming on in the basement, then returned to my room and put on jeans, a sweater over my t-shirt, sneakers that were the only shoes I'd brought home with me from school. On the way back downstairs, I looked out the window on the landing and noted the way snow lined the edges of the window sills next door and the tall, arrow-shaped posts of the fence that created a border between our house and the neighbor's. The snow would be gone by the afternoon but, for now, created a sure settled covering to the ground, as if the snowfall had come from another world. A small scar just above the branch where a circle of ice has formed.

The alleyway was slippery as I made my way up toward 30th and the next stretch of alley that led to Highland Place. The asphalt soon gave way to rocks and stones and I walked up the hill where years ago Iris had fallen after being attacked by a neighbor's dog. There had been no one else around that day, so I had to run down the hill to get my father, who was sitting in his chair outside in the garden and reading his paper. He hadn't come with us to the pool that day and for months after my mother would remark that, had he done so, she wouldn't have been attacked by the dog. There was no way of knowing what would have happened, how things would have evolved that day or any of the days before or after. Just as now, walking past the house, its porch cold and empty in the morning light, the porch swing motionless before the living room windows that looked out onto the street, there was no way to recall a time that wasn't that time, that wasn't made permanent by what had not yet happened but kept happening. My mother, limping from her wounds, my father's face as he saw her lying on the street, her hands covering her leg as blood oozed down through her hands and onto her ankles. And my mother's voice, habitual and sharp, as I made my way up the hill. As it was again my father's eyes looking down that I remembered, his face nearly expressionless, as he leaned down to help Iris, who gazed back up at him, then at me, as if to say, *I'm hurt for god's sake can't you see I'm hurt.*

I would have normally turned around at that point but for some reason kept going, past the grand Victorian homes that had once, in the early part of the 20th century, been the summer residences of Washington's wealthier families. I cut through the nursery school that overlooked Ordway and remembered that I'd broken into the building one night a few years back and found myself standing in the downstairs play area for the pre-kindergarten children who attended the school and roamed through the halls for a good half hour before leaving without taking anything and returning home. The playground was deserted as I continued back past the jungle gym and walked down the hill toward Ordway.

When I came to the corner of Ordway and 30th, I looked down the street and could see the outlines of our house in the middle of the block. Iris stood there waiting for me as I returned from school some days, her hand raised in a half wave as she saw me coming down the hill. There is no structure to the memory, no way to place it. Now becomes then. Then becomes now. Her house coat. Smell of talcum powder. Tobacco and Scotch on her breath. The woman isn't there but is. I'm coming down the hill the way I've always come down the hill. The day after the day after.

The grass edging the sidewalk was crunchy underfoot. I went to the side of the road and stood at the street's edge and played with a line of snow, nudging it with my right foot until it merged with the grass. I came back the way I'd always gone, as if the streets of this neighborhood two days after Christmas were the streets of a childhood that took place long ago, another's life in place of mine, one that had ended with my birth 13 years and a little over eight months ago. There was no way of knowing then what would be. What it would look like when you saw it all over again. How this day was a prologue to other days and the other days future signs of what hadn't yet passed but would. Again and again until the tale no longer made sense, except in fragments shared by strangers.

I was thirteen years-old. It was December 27, 1971. My mother was dead.

FORTY-FIVE

In the months prior to my mother's death, while attending St. Francis Prep in Spring Grove, Pennsylvania, I received one letter from my father, written on October 21, 1971. The letter precedes by a little more than two months my mother's suicide.

>Dear Andy: It was very nice to spend time with you and even to about 50 miles extra to York. If you will now on getting rid of all deficiencies on your report card known to you and all others - - everything will be OK. Mummy is now much more encouraged with my report and is expecting a letter from you. We will write to you before Thanksgiving Day to set out the details of your coming and about everything you should bring with you.
>
>Now few advises: Don't keep my letters to you, rather destroy them! otherwise you can mix them with other papers you bring with you.
>
>For your own interest: don't mention to Mummy anything about thefts in the school; avoid buying <u>anything</u> in shops just not to create the impression that maybe you didn't buy but st.....; buy for me the purse <u>only</u> if they have exactly what I want and in that case take the receipt.
>
>In general, don't buy the present for us; as much as it is sweet, you know that Mummy always can be furious with them later.
>
>Send Mummy a card for birthday Nov. 1; call her on Sunday 31 during the day collect 202 966 3783. You just put in 10c. and dial 0, tell operator what you want and she returns to you 10c. Don't make person to person, just collect to anybody from Andrew.

That's probably all: go to the barber if there is cheaper and buy the trousers only if they are cheaper...

All the best, R

Mummy told me just now by telephone, that she received very sweet letter from you and she is just writing you.

My father's protectiveness of me, combined with his willingness to collude with me in that protectiveness, are what strike me now in this letter written in the face of circumstances that my father must have realized were only getting worse. Destroy his letters or hide them? What was he afraid of? My mother's temper erupting upon her discovery of these secret communications between her husband and their son? It was like a division in the ground, drawn over and over again, so that you had to look to see the line covered over by each new rain. But it was there, the real time offering, and the fear that was lodged in his words. His advice to me not to keep his letters, his caution about my stealing (I recall now that I'd tried to steal a shirt from a clothing store in York, PA, and had been caught by the manager, who in turn had spoken to the headmaster at my school, who had in turn written to my mother and father), the repeated references to money: these concerns stray far, it would seem, from Iris's clearly deteriorating physical and psychological health.

Yet wasn't this all part of the bargain he needed to keep: with me, with himself, to guarantee that Iris would never learn of my father's intentions here, the secrecy and intimacy he wanted to share with me but knew what it would mean to my mother were she to find out? We were secret sharers, he and I, as once my mother and I had been, bearing for each other such protections in the guise of love.

Following my mother's death that December, I would receive many letters from Richard during the next several months I remained at the private Catholic school. Sometimes he would send as many as two or three letters in a week; other times there would be a short note, then nothing for a few weeks. I keep these letters to this day as a record—partial, contingent, discontinuous—of this second phase of our lives together, this period broken off it seemed from the body of the first, my mother's death separating and uniting us in the same instant. The partiality of the record is akin to the ways in which contact was broken, re-started, but continuous nonetheless. I began to realize that, with my mother gone, my father was all I had. The first letter is dated January 12, 1972, and follows Richard's dropping me off at school after the winter break:

Dear Andy: Good morning Mr. Smith. How are you? I came back without difficulties, but the last 20 miles I travelled in rain, dark and terrible fog. It was not pleasant at all, but I still came home in 2 hours. The first night I visited our friends the Sadowskis but now I am spending evenings at home because it is still so much to do. Imagine: your Auntie Gwen wrote to Mrs. Sadowski. Having her address from the old time she was sure that our neighbor Mary, whose name Mums mentions, was she and Gwen thanked her for the help etc. etc. I gave this letter to the proper Mary and explained the funny mistake.
Princess is not very happy that she must wait for me

so long, Sammy doesn't care. But I am giving Princess special treatment when I come back and long walk. She accepted Vitamins without any resistance. Whichever I do & wherever I go I am thinking of you and often speaking to you: "Now we are going to do this, that." Maybe you should do the same and it will help you to have instigation in your studies

Will write again by the end of this week and will send you all the addresses.

Kisses, Tatus   R

1.12.72

Ask Father Robert whether by mistake I didn't write on all the checks year 1971 ?

It is getting again warmer.

His letter was written barely three weeks after Iris's death. The Christmas season had passed. Winter, visits to friends, a quick mention of Mary, a friend of my mother's from her last years, notations about our pets. Normal life, my father seems to say, absolutely normal life. Everything goes on. Sitting on my bunk bed in the room I shared with three other boys, I was struck by the affection in my father's voice, the way he remembered my habit of saying "Now we are going to do this, that," a game we played sometimes before bedtime when I would ask what was coming the next day, and he would say, "Now we are going to do this…" and his voice would trail off and I'd remember that it was a phrase Iris had once shared with me and I'd repeated and hadn't forgotten.

My father's next letter followed a week later:

Andrew. I cannot understand why did you call me, unless you wanted to make me nervous. In all cases like this you must wait and see what happens. Why don't you wait until you are really called to the headmaster and hear from him. May be you lied to me and he has already reprimanded you.

And even so what. <u>They</u> are the teachers and your Masters and you have to listen to them even if you think that they are making mistake. They are not animals...they know what they want and they are responsible for the discipline.

Any kind of complain you should and must tell the headmaster or directly to the teacher asking him for a private talk. Don't call me! I can't help!

And don't you try to act in this way that you think you can convince me to take you from this school. The only alternative would be next year a military school.

So Andrew calm down! Smile and do whatever they tell you even if you think they are wrong.

The normal letter will follow in a few days.

Kisses,

Ry

I can see that 5 mins. after calling me you regretted to do it.

"Don't call me! I can't help!" Strange words to hear from my father, stranger yet to receive them in the midst of our "new" life without Iris. Perhaps he'd understood my stronger wish to be brought home, to live under the same roof where not long ago my mother had taken her life. Perhaps it was just simply what he said: he wouldn't be convinced by any actions of mine meant to have him change plans that had already been made, money that had already been paid. And the hint of understanding resting underneath the anger: "I can see that you after 5 mins. after calling me you regretted to do it."

The "normal letter" would follow, along with others. My life was being lived parallel to Richards, and the letters were some strange, stirring confirmation that I still existed elsewhere, had a home I would return to one day. Walking to Mass each morning at the small chapel where all the freshmen and sophomores gathered, I would sometimes re-read my father's letters, while around me the voices of my classmates rose up into the chapel ceiling:

Hail Mary, full of grace.
The Lord is with thee.
Blessed art thou amongst women,
and blessed is the fruit of thy womb, Jesus.
Holy Mary, Mother of God,
pray for us sinners,
now and at the hour of our death.
Amen.

I didn't know if I was a sinner, suspected that I was, kept reading my father's words so that by the end of Mass I'd re-read the same letter three or four times.

Nights after lights out, I snuck out of the dormitory and went down to the old gymnasium used for storing outdated classroom furniture, old curtain rods and window blinds, a few work benches used for cabinet making and the like. There were a few old post office bikes kept just inside the entryway, ridden once every so often by one of the brothers on their way from one end of campus to the other. I would wheel one of these out of the gym in the darkness and ride down the school driveway to the main road, then down to a flat parking lot about a mile from the school. I'd ride as once José and I had done back in D.C., and I'd remember the sounds of the back alley at night and conjure up some fantasy of riding my bike down the hill, past the smoke shop in town, out to the highway and home. There was nowhere to go and after an hour or so of riding in circles on the macadam surface, I'd head back up the hill toward the school and come back under the wrought iron sign that hung across the stone columns, "St. Francis Preparatory— Founded in 1878."

It made little sense to me, my life as it had come to pass day after day. I got new sneakers every couple of months— Converse high tops—from the campus store, delivered by a truck from York that came up the same driveway I'd ridden down nights before. My father's packages came to the school post office regularly, along with his letters, and I'd store everything carefully in the boxes in which they had been sent in the chest under my bed. Sometimes, my father included books with his packages, miscellaneous titles he thought I might like or that I'd told him about: James Herriot's *All Creatures Great and Small*, Thor Heyerdahl's *Kon-Tiki*, Harriet Beecher Stowe's *Uncle Tom's Cabin*. During study halls at night after dinner, instead of reading one of my school books, I'd hide a copy of one of the books my father had sent me in the folded down pages of another book and read from it as one of the brothers sat in front of the class at his desk, a rosary in his hand as he occasionally looked out across the rows of young boys.

*

Occasionally, my father would acknowledge he had little to say in his letter, was writing it seemed just to keep open this connection that had been shaped by the passing of my mother, yet now, in these letters seemed as well to represent a new effort on my father's part to renew, to keep alive, what was visible in photographs and 16 mm. home movies from my first years in this country: his need to keep me close to him. I don't know what it meant for him to record his world for me as he did, but his letters—like those of my mother—seemed necessary, adamant even in their refusal to let time pass without doing something, saying something:

> Dear Andy. There is nothing special to write about. I have a terrible cold but went to the office and today – Monday – it looks like better. We got a letter with condolence from Mr. and Mrs. Lucero and oral condolences from Bohlen and O'Donell who were away and didn't know anything. Also people living now at Ashmead Pl. called me that they have a lot of letters and cables for me. I went there and couldn't recognize the place: it was a very sentimental visit. Today I went with the lawyer to the court and swore that I would properly administer the money left to us as the custodian of certain minor...Yesterday night we had a storm with lightning and thunders, today it is again warm. Sammy seems to be much better so I must find for him some other meal not dry for variety.

Tuesday, morning. Nothing more so I decided to send this letter.

R

1/25/72

The letter records my father's loneliness, to be sure, even as he doesn't acknowledge so much as hint at his feelings about the changed circumstances of his life with the line: *"it was a very sentimental visit."* What could it have been like for him to go back to the house he and Iris had first shared in Washington, to go there on this journey to pick up mail related to the death of Iris, to stand as he must have stood on that porch and wait for the new owners to come to the door, a pile of mail in their hands to give him, then to walk back down the steps onto the brick pathway and pause there, unsettled, unseen, making his way back to his car and the drive back home again? To find it all the same and all different, as 38 years later I would return with my own daughter, then a little over four years-old, and stand with her on the same front porch of the same house and direct her gaze to the wrought iron window gates over the windows and say to her, "I'll never forget how I used to watch from inside and look for my father when he would pull up in his Chevrolet, right there in front of the house," and have her look where I was looking, for just that time we stood there.

And it could be said, rereading my father's letter in a different time, long separated from that time, that the act of recall formed this odd kind of foreshadowing: that his journey back pre-dating mine made my own return visit inevitable, part of the turning leaves of our history, one day to the next. As if our histories formed a kind of circle, one that begins in one place, drops off, resumes, comes back to another part of the circle. Just as my father would find himself writing me of a visit to the house in which we had spent our first years, so I would re-read his letter years after the fact of his visit and remember that it was surely a gesture of some kind, a back-looking glance he'd made across the garden where there had once been a small plastic swimming pool resting in the grass and a woman sitting by its side in a floral dress, and her hands reaching into the water for her newly arrived infant son.

"We will find the time another day," my father used to say, when I would ask him to let us stay longer someplace, continue a game we'd started, anything that joined us for a period of unbroken time. "We will find the time." Time stopped, then started again. My mother died and time stopped. My father came to find her and time started again. His voice like a whisper that joined the mourning dove's cry, *Znajdziemy czas*. We will find the time.

Did my father (he doesn't say) find in those cables and letters some affirmation, some reconciliation with Iris's death? What must it have meant to him to hear from people he hadn't been in touch with since the post-war years when he and my mother had lived in London together, to read their words of sympathy that must have seemed at once generous and beside the point? Years later when he gave me a box of these cards and cables and letters, I opened it and found inside dozens of cards inscribed in Polish to my father, a few letters in English from mutual friends in London, Paris, Brussels, most from people I'd never heard of and I thought: how strange to have kept these and how many are still alive and who remembers Iris now or their marriage that ended years ago?

At the end of the month, a Saturday, January 29th, I received a much longer letter from my father:

> Dear Andy. Since last Friday for the whole week I have a kind of cold, not a big coughing or catarrh, just always very tired, sweating and changed voice. Since I never had a temperature I did not stay at home but every day going very early to bed, using Vic and all medicines we have at home. Now after 2 days off I feel much better but not entirely perfect. I am still eating at home and even enjoying this. Peggy did not reply whether she will agree to clean our house once a fortnight, so last Thursday I cleaned the whole house and made a big laundry, the first after you left. I decided to close Mums room and mine for a day, so the animals don't go there and it should be easier to keep these rooms clean. Your room is now widely open for animals and Princess has to sleep on your bed on especially prepared for her blankets.
> I sent to you all the material from Record Club. I don't think you should order anything until coming here and comparing the prices with Discount Sh. Enclosed find please 2 fotos, the custom made is still not ready. I still don't understand why you didn't take the original: they are better and same measure.
> Don't be discourage with the rejecting of your letter to the editor. I think your kind of writing doesn't concur with this style of paper: you are rather critical, witty, satirical. They are editors and decide about the liner of the paper. Maybe in the future you will try to write something serious to try your possibilities in this field.

I don't write about the exams since we have to wait few days until we know the results. But I know this time that you really worked very hard.

As I told you already, you left a cap from your coat. Will bring you this and other. We had only sight snow one evening, but another one, bigger, is forecast for tomorrow. The temp. changed from day to day. One day as I was looking a little more on TV as news / 2 hours: Cronkite and LBJ and The American Justice / I decided to risk and made a fire. Believe or not, whether it was a miracle I don't know - - it was a success: I used two logs and had a fire going on for 4 hours.

I ordered two books from the Book Club: Wheels and Do you sincerely want to be rich? the true story of how Bernard Cornfeld turned a few hundred dollars into a multi-billion dollar empire and lost everything.

If you ever intend to call me, OK, but try to do it after 5 p.m. [Saturday and Sunday no difference the whole day in price.] OK?

So for the moment enough.

Love
Ry

Our flight to London is June 21 to July 11, I already sent a deposit
$200.

The following month, two more letters came. My father seemed to have found his correspondence with me a way to focus on the mundane, the everyday and observable. Lying awake in my bunk bed at school, I often imagined his passage through his days and nights, portions of which were related in his letters to me. And I would see him in his torn dressing gown emerging from room after room, like the refugee he'd once been, and his hands would be blue from cold and his eyes shiny from tears. And he would enter each room of the house all over again, opening and closing all the doors, until he stood in her room again and opened the window and let the cold winter air in and sat underneath it, near the cold radiator, and dried his eyes with the edge of his gown.

But he did not cry, not in his letters to me nor, do I imagine, in those long nights he spent alone in our house. No, he wrote simply of what he knew, what he could hold and touch and see around him: our "animals," the newly fallen snow, invitations to dinner, a proposed trip to England in June and later a trip to the Maryland shore.

On February 2nd, he wrote me the following letter:

> Hello Andy. I am writing on Wednesday night from the office. Yesterday, when I returned home around 1 am, the weather was clear and temp above freezing. When about 7:30 am I went to the WC, everything was covered with snow. But around noon the snow changed into rain and the first snow quickly disappeared. I didn't even have very much bother with cleaning the steps. Princess and Sammy liked this first snow. Now, as usually, they went to sleep and will wake up when I will be back asking for food. Peggy called me that she is very busy and at least for the time being she cannot work for us. It is quite possible that I will still manage to do everything by myself. This coming weekend I will have guests from London: they will stay at the hotel but I will spend much of my time with them and already have invitation for 2 dinners. Next week also

somebody is coming from NY, but the weekend after next, Sunday 20 February, I am spending with my little boy in Hanover or York. The next day is Washington Birthday and I am not working but you – I presume – have a regular school day. As you already know we going to England on June 21 to July 11. I am taking also another week in August so we would be able to go together to the beach. Everything depends whether you will need to take any summer course. We will discuss everything when we meet. Is there anything I should bring with me? I received today another bill from Princess Laundry. I hope you started new semester with good will to work and I am waiting for the report although I know already from you what is in.

Keep smile and love

R

The next letter, dated Sunday, February 20, was written the day my father was to have visited me at St. Francis. A heavy snowstorm prevented my father from visiting his "little boy" and delivering in person his package of figs, cookies and other foodstuffs I had told him I wanted. I wouldn't see him again until later that spring when he came to collect me and bring me home for the beginning of our new life together at Ordway Street.

My mother had been dead a little over two months by this point. There is little in my father's tone here to indicate that loss. It is, rather, an inventory of observable facts, the world as my father had come to know it, living between his caretaking of me from a distance of a couple hundred miles and his forming sense of a life without Iris.

Dear Andrew. This is the time I should arrive to your place. Instead I am sitting still in my pajamas after leaving the warm bed when Princess is still covered with plenty of blankets. Sammy is sitting next to me and the radiator. The temp. outside is 25, the sun just appeared but the wind is about 40 m/h. One hear it all the time and the feeling is not nice at all. You see the trees bending, it looks like the whole house will be drifting together with snow. I have just called the AAA, as I was doing all the day yesterday: Nothing to regret my decision: the roads north to Fredericksburg are mostly closed or dangerous and the Penn Police warned against unnecessary driving as the snow is still falling down. So this is our life: First and maybe the last winter blizzard came exactly when I was about to visit you. As a matter of fact also I am working 4 hours tonight because of President Nixon arrival to Peking. My next Sunday off is March 5 and I expect to see you in your place around 10:30-11 am. The fact that I am working nearly every Sunday is very good: we both need money and the more I can earn, the better. Speaking about money I hope you still have enough in your bank. If not, write. The first snow falled down here on Thursday, when I returned from the office. On Friday, I was off, it was clear and warmer so I had no difficulties with cleaning the snow from the front, back and the car. Later it rained terribly all the time but on Saturday morning it was snow, wind, cold and I started being afraid that I would be not able to go. And so happened.

Now...I am sending on Tuesday you the envelope with everything I can put there, except the food I bought for you: fig cookies, apples, oranges, chocolates.

Yesterday, I cleaned again the whole house including the kitchen, the oven and the kitchen floor. Sammy was bleeding terribly and I took him to the vet last Friday. He got special peels 3 times a day which he is taking very easy; probably understanding that he needs them. Joanna showed me the letter you wrote to her. Your mother's sisters, Gwen and Memsie, wrote to me telling they wrote to you but they don't expect the reply knowing you are very busy. The school sent me again the form for you joining the special reading courses. I ignore it because you were very good with your test. They probably know it and this is only routine? But ask, just in case.

I hope you would be able to visit Keims if the weather changes. I enclose the letter to the school. If you visit them, call me collect from their place on Saturday night between 8 and 9. That is all.

Kindest regards
Love
R

Princess likes the snow and goes very often to the garden in her red clothes. In few hours time I am taking her to mail this letter and then to clean a little the front from the snow and to prepare the car for my night journey to the office.
I made fire 4 times and every time it was a success. I cleaned the fire place every time.

I cannot say with certainty, but my father seemed in this administering to daily tasks—sweeping the snow from the front of the house, walking Princess to the post office, and so on—to have been recognizing the significance in his life of those tasks and routines without which he had little hold on life. And the direction of his words to me, their slipping in and out of the ordinary: as if to break from such forms would be to risk sanity itself.

"Were you happy finally, knowing you didn't have to worry about Iris anymore?" I would ask.

"No," he said, "I was living my life to exist, that is all. To take care of you. That's all."

The commonest task made to seem in its own way a kind of redemption, a form of clarity, before which he could rest, pleased with his accomplishments: *I made fire 4 times and every time it was a success. I cleaned the fire place every time.*

*

The photograph has darkened, the light dull and orange at the edges of the frame. A man with a film camera faces the photographer, while to his left a woman in her early 40's holds a baby in diapers in her arms. The weather would seem to be spring, though one can't say for certain. The expression on the woman's face is one of outward joy. The baby has turned his head to face the camera and, just before the photograph is taken, the family friend taking the photograph calls out, "Andy! Andy! Look at the camera, Andy!"

The awning next door has been unfolded to protect against afternoon sun. The new mother and her son have gone back inside the house. The father waits on the porch with their friend to enter the house, turns, sees the light lowering across the trees. From inside the house the father hears the cries of his year-old son.

"Tak," he says, "Yes. Time to go inside."

EPILOGUE: ANGELIKI'S LETTERS

'The same thing over and over again,' you'll tell me, friend.
But the thinking of a refugee, the thinking of a prisoner, the thinking of a person when he too has become a commodity—
try to change it; you can't.
                George Seferis, "Logbook II"

In 1994 I began a correspondence with representatives of International Social Service (ISS) in New York, the organization that had helped arrange my adoption in 1959. I wrote that I was seeking any information they could provide me about the whereabouts of Angeliki Sakkas. I didn't even bother to inquire about the whereabouts of my father. In the early spring of 1995 I was contacted by an agent from ISS and informed that my mother was indeed still alive, and welcomed the news of my existence. My mother's hand-written letter in Greek followed later that year, translated by a caseworker in Athens:

> Athens, 12.4.1995
> My beloved child, I am in good health and I wish the same to you, to be always well.
> My dear child, when I received your letter, I felt an indescribable happiness, mostly because I learned that you are well.
> This letter is difficult for me to write, as it was for you.
> I felt a great happiness and excitement that after so many years, I was able to find you. My boy, all these years I was thinking of you but I didn't know your whereabouts. the only thing I knew, when they took you, was that you would go to USA, but I didn't know the area.
> Some time ago, the Social Service phoned me and told to go to their office in order to inform me about a personal matter. First, they went to the village where I come from, and communicated with my sister in order to learn where I live. Then my sister gave them my address and phone number and after they contacted me, we started a discussion for you, my son.
> For me, the mother that gave birth to you, it was really difficult to give you to other hands, but unfortunately, there

was no other way, my son. Since your father abandoned me and didn't marry me, it was really difficult for me to raise you and to offer you the necessary education, in order for you to become a good man in society. I was poor and I could not offer you all these that your adoptive parents offered you. I would really like to thank them because they were good persons, they raised you in the right way and gave you the necessary education in order for you to become a good man. And now, we are all proud of you.

My son, you should love your adoptive father, because he, as well as your adoptive mother, raised you from a very young age and they heard your crying and worries. Your adoptive parents themselves would have a lot of worries, because a child does not grow up without worries.

You wrote to me that your adoptive mother has died. I am sure that she offered you a lot and you should go and light a candle for her, who was such a good person.

Although I take a pension, my son, I continue to work, because pensions in Greece are very low and the cost of living is high. Here in Greece, we have great unemployment and young persons cannot find work easily. Others also, who have work are not able to face every day expenses.

My dear child, you wrote to me you had come to Greece in 1990, and were looking for me. But at that time, there were no telephones in my village, that is why you could not find me.

You wrote to me my son, that you are in love with a girl. If she is good, marry her, do not cheat and leave her. After you finish your studies, marry her and come with her to Greece. I will be very happy to see you, my child. And after so many years, I will see you as a young man, that you are now. When you come to Greece, we'll say more.

I wish you my son to find the job you want, after you

finish your studies. I wish with all my heart that God will help you to find everything you want in your life.

My son, Andreas, you have your birthday in April 20th, and I wish you to live like "the high mountains" and God to give you all the best.

Now, my son, I kiss you with great happiness and excitement. I, your mother Angeliki, send you many kisses and all my love. My son, Andreas, whenever you are able, I will be waiting for you to hold you in my arms. I would wish myself to be a bird, in order to fly and come to you my son and see you, and then come back again.

My son, I send you many kisses and the wish to see you soon.

A few months later, another letter from my mother arrived, again with a translation by a caseworker from ISS Athens: This one would be undated, typed on plain bond, folded into fours:

My beloved and unforgettable child Andrew,
I am fine, as far as my health is concerned, and I wish the same for you.
Be always well my son Andrew, and I'm fine too.
I received your letter and my happiness was indescribable. I wish you to be always well like the "high mountains," I'm still working. What can I do my son? Life is very expensive. How can we manage? We should work until 100 years of age. Here in Greece, there is great unemployment and if someone has a big family, then at least 4 persons should work in order to be able face everyday expenses. The rents are very high. A two-room apartment costs 60,000 drachmas per month and if you add electricity, water, etc., then you need over 100,000 drachmas per month. If you count also the expenses for food, you can understand why I'm still working. I'll work until I will be able, then I'll stop. I already feel tired as I've worked since I was 8 years old.
In our village, we didn't have much land and therefore my family couldn't manage.
I was working like a man in order to help my family. My mother died when she was 40 years old. At that time my sister was 4 years old and I was responsible for her, also.
My father died when he was 65 years old.
My brother went with the guerillas at the mountains in order to fight Germans who invaded our country. Then the civil war was started and the one "brother" killed the other. The one "brother" was with the guerillas and the

other was at the army and they killed each other.

The civil war ended in 1948 and at that time others got away in Poland, others in Soviet Union, others in Czechoslovakia and others in Hungary. Many Greeks had been dispersed in all East countries, as that time was very difficult for the communists.

There was much hate among people and due to fascism many people were killed, especially the guerillas who were fighting for freedom and independence.

The guerillas were imprisoned and exiled. Many of them were taken during the night and executed. Do you understand now, my child, why your uncle is living in Poland? He was forced to leave his wife and child and go to another country. In Poland, he married for the second time and made a new family.

The circumstances were such that my brother couldn't return to Greece and therefore, I was the one who faced all the difficulties, my child. I have passed so many difficulties in my life, that if I were a writer I would write a book. I had enough of work, both to my village and Athens. I worked as a cleaning woman in houses, where my employers didn't let me go out, not even to the movies.

My dear child, Andreas, it is very hot, here. But what can we do? It's summer and we'll suffer, somehow.

Well, my dear child, I do not have anything else to write you. I kiss you with many kisses.

Andreas, my child, I'm looking forward to receive your letter, the soonest possible.

I kiss you again with many kisses and I'm waiting for you and your wife, during autumn.

I send many kisses to your wife and your dear father and I wish you from my heart to finish your studies at the university, soon.

> I wish you farewell till we meet in Greece.
> I kiss you all,
> Your mother

I let the silence go uninterrupted for weeks, then months. A year passed. My mother's letters and cards arrived as if we had followed the course of our lives together, as if I could impart some language that would redress her wound that had opened again. "Let the speech that knows no lie," Odysseus Elytis has written, "recite my mind out loud." I wanted to recite out loud the letters from my Greek mother, to put them next to those that remained from Iris, to ask of one, then the other, *How can this be, how did this happen?* that one claimed me, but didn't want me; the other wanted but couldn't keep me. Birth mother and adoptive mother, fused, not fused, echoing each other in their son's life, so that what I could ask, what I couldn't ask of either, of each of them, lay inside the words they spoke and wrote me. And the violence of one was tended by the gentleness of another, and if I looked back to one I must have looked ahead to another, awaiting me, as if she were the one I had sought all my life, without reason or understanding except that which blood gave me.

In May 1999, a little over a year after the birth of my first daughter, Mia, I received this letter from Angeliki, addressed to both Madeline, my wife at the time and mother of my two children, and me:

> My dearest children, Andrew and Madeline,
> I'm fine and wish the same for you. My dear children, I received your letter and photographs. You cannot imagine my happiness seeing Mia growing up and coming a

little girl. Whenever she starts saying words, she will be marvelous. I wish her to live like high mountains. I wish you also to another child, as they will both have company and play with each other. It will be different.

As you know, my Andrea, the war in Serbia is very near us and we don't know how it will end. For 3 months now, they bomb Serbia and kill small children. But it's not these children's fault. These children don't know anything about life yet. I don't understand how they can kill children. They don't have children themselves? They will regret it one day, but then it will be late.

My dear children, I'm still working, although I have problems with my legs. My doctor, who is a very good man and doesn't ask me to pay him, has given me some ointments, which I use.

My Andrea, I don't write you more. Your cousin Agatha sends you her best regards.

I'm waiting for your letter. Write to me about your father. How is he?

I kiss you all with many kisses.

Your mother

One of the last letters I received from Angeliki is dated March 5, 2001:

My dearest son Andreas,

I am fine and I wish the same for you all. I am very sorry my Andreas that I couldn't write to you earlier. I asked the social worker to write you a letter because I couldn't write myself as I had an eye operation. Now I am fine and after Easter I'll make the same operation to the other eye. It is an operation for eye cataract. It is not so serious but after the operation I have to be careful for sometime. I must no to any kind of work and mostly I must not bend down.

My Andreas, write to me how are the children and your wife. How things are going with your work at the University? Write to me about your father.

I don't know what is happening with the earthquakes. I've heard that there was a strong one in U.S.A. but I don't know if it was near where you live. The earthquake is one of the worst things that happen as people may lose their lives and others their property.

My Andreas, write to me a letter because I worry about you. I would like to know about you all.

I will not write you more. I kiss you all with many kisses.

I am looking forward to receiving your letter, the soonest possible.

    With all my love,
        your mother

I wrote back infrequently after our initial contact, sometimes taking several months before I responded. This letter, dated 26 October 2002, nearly five months after Madeline and I had separated and I had taken a job at Shippensburg University in Shippensburg, PA, is one of the few letters I kept and was written more than a year after my mother's March 2001 letter:

Dear Mother –

A long long time without word from me. I'm terribly sorry, but things have been very difficult in my new life here in Pennsylvania. I have gotten hired as a tenure track faculty member in English at a small university south of

Harrisburg. The job is, as they say, the job of my dreams, but the work has required me to leave my home and children in New Jersey – very very difficult. I speak to my girls every night, yet of course it's not the same as actually being able to spend time with them, watch them grow daily, etc. Every two weeks they come down for a weekend, and we have wonderful times, going to the park, playing in my apartment, etc., lovely lovely hours when I can just be with them and not have any distractions...

The job is, as I said, near-perfect in terms of my aspirations, ambitions and so on...I teach poetry and poetry writing, along with classes in composition (required of all students), and the department is by and large a friendly one. Unfortunately, so far I've been unable to make much of a life for myself outside of work, but this will no doubt happen in time. Essentially, for now, my days are spent driving to the university (25 minutes from where I live), teaching, meeting students in my office, doing work at the school, then driving back in late afternoon. I had some friends here for a time at the beginning, but those relationships became soured for reasons I won't go into. So now I am pretty much by myself...

I think of you often, dear mother....I know it is hard when I do not write you more often, but as I said my life here has been a mixed blessing. Whatever extra time I've had, I've tried to spend with my children. In addition, I recently moved my 92 year-old father to a Catholic nursing home in Baltimore. He seems content there, has his own room, and is able to speak Polish once again to the mostly Polish staff. Odd to say, but he will no doubt spend the remainder of his days in this place.

Mother, I hope you are well. I embrace you with all my heart, and send hugs and kisses to you and everyone in our family. Write when you are able and send any new photographs you may have (I have enclosed some of my girls, and one self-portrait of your son...)

love,

Andrew

Separation, abandonment, children left without parents, parents without children....I wouldn't have been able to understand at this time of writing Angeliki how the circumstances of her life and my own were replicating certain aspects of each other's life experience, demands that had been placed on each of us in different ways for different reasons, now come full circle it seemed. I don't know if I hoped for advice from Angeliki on how to be a better father where there had been no such man present in her life when she made the decision she felt she had to make so early in her own life. Writing Angeliki so distant from the life I had called my own, now separated from that life and that of my daughters, I could only imagine that I must be another disappointment to the soul of this Greek mother who wanted such good things for the children she called her own.

*

The last letter I received from Angeliki was addressed from Athens, December 8th, 2002:

My dearest Andrea,
We are all fine and I hope the same for you.
A long time passed without a word from you -almost a

year. I felt really sorry about that but now that I received your letter and photographs, I cannot describe my happiness.

My Andrea, you write to me that you moved to another place but your wife and children left behind. My Andrea, wherever is better for you. Continue to write to me about your wife and children, give them many kisses and tell them that I love them very much.

Well, my Andrea, I send you 3 photographs. I don't know if you like them. The two of them are from the house of your aunt Eleni in the village, during Easter. The third one is from your cousin Makis' marriage in Athens. I want to tell you also that your cousin Agathi got engaged.

My Andrea, I'm glad that your father feels fine in the new nursing home. Write me more about him, as well as about your job and your children.

Your uncle (my brother) lives in Poland with his daughter.

My Andrea, I will not write you more. I kiss you all with many kisses . Have a nice time during holidays. Merry Christmas and a Happy New Year.

I'm waiting for your letter. I Kiss you all.

With all my love,
Your mother

*

When my mother's letters stopped arriving in 2005, I wrote to ISS again, requesting information about my mother's condition. She hadn't been well, suffering from phlebitis and other ailments, for which she apparently was scheduled to undergo an operation. In December 2006, three years after my father's death and after nearly a year of silence from my mother, I learned from the caseworker who'd been handling the case that Angeliki had died in February of 2005 in Athens, two years after Richard. The direct cause of death was complications from phlebitis, though Angeliki hadn't been well for a number of years apparently, with little access to the kind of medical care that might have made a difference. No other details were available to me and the caseworker indicated that Angeliki's immediate family in Greece had requested that I have no further contact with their family.

That winter I was, for the first time in my life, without parents.

*

In the artifice of memory, Angeliki is standing before me again on the black surface of a road in the bright noon day sun. Her body is clothed in black and she is wearing a gold necklace with a crucifix. In her hand is a book of poems she has brought out to read to me. The pages are marked with signs, leafy drawings she made when she was a child. I walk in the middle of the road, no traffic, a hot day, one of the hottest in years they had reported in the local paper. In the distance the fields, yellow, darkening, and beyond them a row of mountains I can imagine as they must have appeared to my mother when I was a child. "Angeliki," I say. She doesn't, at first, acknowledge me. Then a smile, slow, deliberate, and her eyes open wide in greeting.

"My young son from the mountains," she says to me, "you have come to find me. You have come back to your old mother and found her."

The sun is close to the treetops and level with my eyes as I take her in, as she takes my body into hers. There is lightness in her touch and the scent of olive wood and jasmine.

"Angeliki," I say, "Your son from the mountains has come home to find you."

In a small cemetery outside Liknon, a flat stone marks the site of my mother's grave and bears the inscription: Αγγελική Σακκά 1932-2005. I am told that in the spring the fields nearby are awash in color from the poppies and wild roses that return each year and the olive groves fill the air with the lush fragrance of ash and cinnamon.

ACKNOWLEDGMENTS

In a book that has taken the better part of two decades to complete, I owe more than I could ever say to the many individuals who accompanied me on this journey and gave of their time, attention and careful reflection as I sought to bring into the world the story of Angeliki, Richard and Iris and the childhood I shared with and apart from them. I can only mention a limited number of these individuals below, though others will recognize their contributions here and have my deepest thanks for their participation in the journey this book has represented.

Portions of this work first appeared in somewhat different form in *New Ohio Review* and *Ergon: Greek/American Arts and Letters*. Grateful acknowledgment to Catherine Taylor and Yiorgos Anagnostou, the respective editors of these publications, for their support of this project.

Thanks to Hank Lazer, who understood the stakes of this project for me from the beginning and to Paul Naylor, whose friendship and responses to this work during its initial stages of writing made all the difference between producing a book and a stack of disconnected pages. His careful reading of and responses to drafts of this project have been substantive in ways I can only begin to acknowledge here.

For hours spent at their kitchen table in Silver Spring, Maryland, listening again to stories of my father, reviewing his history and ours together, my thanks and love to Anna, Tadeusz and Emma Zachurski. Their presences are folded into these stories that they helped me to tell those many days and nights ago spent in what came to feel like my second home.

I owe profound debt of gratitude to Bradford Morrow for his care for and publishing portions of this work in somewhat different form in the literary bi-annual, *Conjunctions*. His encouragement at various points along the way as I returned to this project was invaluable and sustaining in ways that truly made the difference between completing this work and not.

Special thanks to Rachel Blau DuPlessis, who was one of the earliest readers of writing that would eventually find its way into this book and who read and commented on multiple, early drafts of this manuscript as it took shape. Her enthusiasm for and support of this project and the related poem projects that were being written alongside this work remained pivotal and decisive.

Likewise, to Rachel Tzvia Back, who carried the pages of a much earlier version of this book back to Israel with her in 2008 and has continued to read drafts as they've come to her, I owe a profound debt of gratitude. Rachel's careful reading and re-reading and comments borne from her own career and work as a poet, literary scholar and translator provided important notes in this book's final stages of writing.

In a book that is invested in and deeply engaged by the documentary, getting access to early records of my time at Metera and other documents in my file held by International Social Services was a critical and relatively late addition to the writing of this work. For help in retrieving these documents and for critical information on Greek life in the 1950's and early 1960's, I am deeply grateful to Gonda Van Steen. Her important study, *Adoption, Memory, and Cold War Greece: Kid pro quo?*, came at a pivotal time in late revisions of this book and genuinely made this version of the story possible in the way it's presented here. Gonda's help in retrieving documents from ISS gave me access to an archive of materials related to my adoption that I quite simply would not have had without her assistance and pointing me in the right direction. Her guidance and assistance in translations of letters from Angeliki and her firsthand knowledge of adoption practices in Greece at the time of my adoption, as well as the social contexts related thereto, have been incorporated into this version of the book, without which significant portions of the tale as represented here couldn't have been told.

To Tod Thilleman, my editor at Spuyten Duyvil Press, who read this book in both its wayward and more directed drafts, I owe a world of thanks, for believing in this project and understanding that it really was the book that needed to come out next. His dedication and attentiveness to this project across the many years of our friendship as he published other books of mine have been signally important. Here's to many more books to follow!

The writing process that resulted in this memoir is one that has been from the beginning inextricably intertwined with my own developing understanding of fatherhood—both my own and that of my father, Richard. In ways that perhaps will not be meaningful to them until years from now, my daughters, Mia and Isabel, have been central to this book and the narrative arc it represents. Their stories are found here as well, in the intricate layers of lost histories, displacement, and familial lore that are integral to what these pages seek to reveal. If I have learned anything of value from writing this book, it has been in part through raising my own children who have taught me the true and full meaning of the phrase, "We do what we know." To which must be added: And sometimes we learn to do things differently.

Finally, I owe the greatest debt of gratitude to my wife, Monica Jacobe, whose decades-long experience as a writer of creative nonfiction and editor are evident on every page of this work. Mentored by the late Richard McCann (*Mother of Sorrows*) in the MFA program at American University, Monica understood in ways I didn't how our core stories are shaped early and irresolutely and require a combination of ethical imagining and resourceful telling to live again in the narratives we tell. Monica's editorial acumen, tireless reading of and contributions to this work across a decade made the difference between having a book worth reading and a stack of pages. In a project that has been from the beginning about finding love as much as losing it, I am thankful beyond words for Monica's presence in a life too long given over to the latter and failing, until relatively recently, to hold dearly to the former. This book is shared with her in deepest gratitude and love.

ANDREW MOSSIN completed his B.A. in English at Hampshire College and moved to New York City shortly afterward. Living on the Upper West Side of Manhattan, he got his first job as a salesclerk at the recently opened Shakespeare & Co. at 81st and Broadway, after which he worked in arts service organizations in the city (Poets & Writers, The Council of Literary Magazines and Presses) and served under the late Jason Shinder as Managing Director of The Writer's Voice of the West Side YMCA. In 1989, he moved to Philadelphia, where over the next decade he would complete his M.A. in Creative Writing and Ph.D. in English at Temple University. Mossin is currently an Associate Professor in the Intellectual Heritage Program at Temple University and a visiting faculty member in the Language & Thinking Program at Bard College. He lives in Doylestown, PA with his wife, Monica Jacobe.